A CONCISE HISTORY OF ITALY

IONAS

A CONCISE HISTORY OF
ITALY

PETER GUNN

with 231 illustrations

THAMES AND HUDSON · LONDON

For Miranda and Simon

Frontispiece: Jonah. Fresco by Michelangelo
in the Sistine Chapel, Vatican.

Printed and bound in Great Britain by Jarrold and Sons Ltd Norwich

ISBN 0 500 45010 2

Contents

Chapter One

THE DISSOLUTION OF THE ROMAN EMPIRE OF THE WEST, AD 476–568

At the time of the greatest territorial expansion of Rome, in the third century AD, throughout the vast area extending from Scotland to the deserts of Africa and from the Caspian to the Atlantic, the heterogeneous populations were linked in a uniform political organization. Within frontiers guarded by the imperial legions the Roman citizen enjoyed the blessings of the *pax Romana*. Gibbon described the era of the Antonines (the second century AD) as that 'period in the history of the world during which the condition of the human race was most happy and prosperous'.

Yet on the death of the philosopher-emperor Marcus Aurelius in AD 180 a century of anarchy followed, when the state, weakened within, was threatened

Scene, showing Roman legionaries repulsing barbarians, from the Arch of Constantine. Second century AD.

Aureus of the
Emperor Diocletian,
c. AD 290, obverse and
(*below*) reverse.

on its northern frontiers by Franks, Alamanni and Goths, and in the east by the Persians, revived under the Sassanid dynasty. The accession of the Emperor Diocletian in 284 brought about some respite. His reforms in the civil administration of the empire relegated Italy to provincial status; for the first time the inhabitants were subject to the land tax. Italy was subdivided into seventeen 'provinces', each administered by a governor and a hierarchy of lesser officials. The primary aim of the government was to meet from taxation the expenses of the imperial court and the legions, which consisted more and more of barbarian mercenaries.

Nevertheless, even Diocletian's important economic and social measures failed to reinvigorate a moribund society. Municipal life, which once flourished so strongly throughout the empire, decayed. In the countryside the peasantry were sinking to the position almost of serfs; large areas of fertile land went out of cultivation or were unproductively worked by slaves and day labourers. After 330, when Constantine the Great founded his administrative capital at Byzantium, which he renamed Constantinople, Italy was but one of the four prefectures, with the Orient, Illyricum and Gaul.

A Council of the Church of
Constantinople. Miniature from
the *Sermons of St Gregory of Nazianzus*
(329–89).

Left. Portrait head of the Emperor Diocletian (284–305). *Right:* The Emperor Constantine the Great (*c.* 312–37).

By the Edict of Milan (313) Constantine legalized the Christian religion, so that thenceforth the Church could accept bequests and legacies. The status of the bishop of Rome had been enhanced by the removal of the imperial administration to Constantinople. The Roman pontiff, as the successor of St Peter, was early recognized as *primus inter pares* by the bishops of Antioch and Alexandria; at the Council of Constantinople (381) the bishop of 'New Rome' was ranked next to the occupant of the older see. Later the bishop of Jerusalem, the mother church of Christendom, was also designated 'patriarch', but as early as 344 an important doctrinal question was referred by an ecumenical council to the decision of the bishop of Rome.

Within Italy the hierarchy developed along the lines of the civil administration. All the larger towns (*civitates*) had their bishops, who were grouped together in provinces under a 'metropolitan'. Later the area of episcopal jurisdiction became known by the originally civil division of 'diocese'. It was only gradually that the Roman episcopate developed into the papacy, claiming supremacy over the entire Christian Church. It was with the breakdown of the civil administration under the incursions of barbarians that the social importance of the bishops (with their subordinate clergy), and especially of the bishop of Rome, became evident. At their disposal were the accumulated riches of the Church, which were used originally for the relief of the poor (*patrimonium pauperum*).

9

The Barbarian Invasions The great migration of peoples from central Asia, westward and southward in direction, impelled from the rear by tribes even more savage and barbarous than themselves, kept up a constant pressure on the northern frontiers of the empire. Theodosius I (*c*. 346–95), who temporarily united East and West, was succeeded by his sons: Arcadius (395–408), who governed the East from Constantinople, and Honorius (395–423) in Italy, who was recognized as Roman emperor of the West. Increasingly both emperors were forced to rely on barbarian mercenaries. One of these, the Vandal general Stilicho, was first the guardian, then the father-in-law of Honorius. With the connivance of the Eastern court, Alaric and his Visigoths (the western branch of the Gothic nation) plundered Illyricum and Greece, until their incursions were checked

Left: The Vandal general Stilicho. Ivory relief from the treasury of Monza Cathedral.

Right: The church of S. Vitale, Ravenna, 526–47, showing mosaics on the vaults and domes.

by Stilicho (396). Shortly after, they crossed into Italy, but were again met by
Stilicho and defeated at Pollentia (402), whereupon they retired beyond the
Alps.

On the murder of Stilicho (Honorius had reason to fear his power) Alaric
recrossed the Alps into Italy, and after being bought off on two occasions,
finally in 410 took Rome and put it to the sack, sparing only the churches. At
the time of the Gothic invasions Honorius shifted his own capital from Milan
to Ravenna, which lent itself more easily to landward defence and to succour
from the sea.

Seal of Alaric, c. 410.

Solidus of Pope Leo I (440–61).

The brief rule (425–40) of Galla Placidia, as Augusta, empress of the West, and regent for her son, Valentinian III, was a period of internal peace, to which the architecture and Byzantine mosaics of Ravenna (notably the mausoleum of Galla Placidia herself) bear testimony. But there now appeared another threat in the north from a people so barbaric that by comparison Alaric's Visigoths seemed civilized. In 452 the king of the nomadic Huns, Attila, crossed the Alps and devastated the cities of northern Italy. Aquileia was sacked (some survivors may have sought refuge in the lagoons, where later Venice was to rise); Padua, Verona, Vicenza, Bergamo suffered likewise; probably also Milan and Pavia. The Emperor Valentinian fled to Rome and dispatched envoys, including the bishop of Rome, Leo I, to treat with Attila. At Lake Garda Attila was persuaded by a large bribe and, according to Church historians, by the dignity and eloquence of the Pope, to retire north.

After Attila's death in 453 the great Hunnish empire rapidly disintegrated; but a new threat soon arose from another quarter. In 455 Gaiseric (or Genseric), the king of the Vandals, landed with his troops at Ostia, having crossed from Africa, and on this occasion not even the eloquence of Pope Leo saved Rome from the plunder of its transportable treasures.

From the death of Valentinian III in 455 (he was assassinated) until the deposition of Romulus Augustus in 476, nine emperors 'successively disappeared', as Gibbon puts it. Military dictators, such as Ricimer (who sacked Rome in 472, the third sack it suffered in some sixty years), made and unmade emperors. In 475 one of these barbarian tyrants, Orestes, a Pannonian, deposed the Emperor Julius Nepos, replacing him by his own son, 'a youth recommended only for his beauty', Romulus Augustulus, as he was derisively known. Orestes refused to meet the demand of the barbarian mercenaries for a grant of one-third of the land of Italy. As a result the Scyrrian (or Herulian) contingents of these troops rose in revolt under their chieftain Odoacer, overcame and slew Orestes, and forced the youthful emperor to retire to a villa on the Bay of Naples (476). With him was extinguished the Western branch of the imperial line.

Outwardly Odoacer respected Roman institutions; he retained the senate and the imperial officials, employing the latter for the purpose of the legal and fiscal administration. He fulfilled his promise to his troops by appropriating the imperial domains and parcelling out the abandoned countryside. The Roman aristocracy for the most part retained their large estates (*latifundia*), apparently undisturbed by the demise of the Western empire; the condition of the classes beneath them also seems to have been little affected. In the towns the bishops appeared as the mouthpiece (*defensores*) of the poorer classes in mitigating the harshness of the ruling minority, whether barbarian or Roman.

The policy of Odoacer and his Gothic successors in their attempts to secure a stable Italian kingdom was based on three paramount objectives: the removal, once the establishment was effected, of the most serious causes of friction between races (a complete fusion, which was desired by both Odoacer, and after him, Theodoric, as well as by far-seeing Romans such as Cassiodorus, was soon found to be impossible); the maintenance of relations with the Eastern emperors which, if not positively that of their acceptance of the *fait accompli*, were not actively hostile; and the support, or at least the neutrality, of the Church.

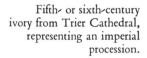

Fifth- or sixth-century ivory from Trier Cathedral, representing an imperial procession.

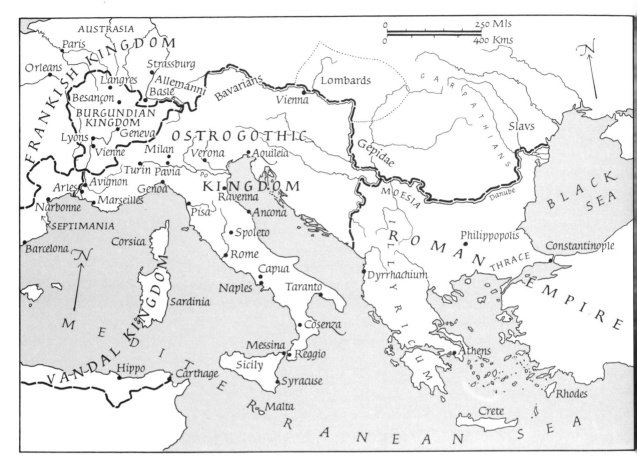

Italy in about AD 525.

The Eastern emperor, Zeno, looked on Odoacer as a usurper, but the Ostrogothic threat to the security of the Eastern empire prevented his taking military action to restore imperial rule in Italy. As an act of political expediency the emperor invested the Ostrogothic chieftain, Theodoric, with the titles of patrician and consul and persuaded him, if he needed persuasion, to lead his Goths over the Julian Alps to regain Italy for the empire. The war opened in 489; Odoacer desperately defended his kingdom and it was not until 493 that Ravenna capitulated. The Eastern emperors at first refused Theodoric's request for confirmation of his title to rule Italy. Meanwhile, his soldiers had proclaimed him king; and it was in reality on his leadership of the Gothic army that he based his sovereignty. As a counterpoise to the enmity of the Eastern

14

emperors, Theodoric sought dynastic marriages with the barbarian rulers of the West: his sister married the king of the Vandals, one daughter the king of the Visigoths, and another the son of the king of the Burgundians, while he himself took for a second wife a daughter of Clovis, the powerful king of the Franks.

In the early and middle years of his long reign (493–526) Theodoric's internal policy met with a measure of success. He confiscated the lands granted by Odoacer to his soldiers and partitioned them out among his own troops, but appropriated no further territory. Towards the senate he showed at first a deference hardly in accord with that body's political impotence. In Rome he revived the decaying schools of art, rhetoric, medicine and law; he issued regulations for the preservation of public buildings and memorials of the imperial past, and repaired aqueducts, walls and cloacae. He was a great builder of palaces and churches. In Ravenna S. Apollinare Nuovo, part of S. Spirito (the baptistery of the Arians) and Theodoric's own mausoleum are evidence of his activity. Agriculture, industry and trade all received stimulus from his policy; he drained an area of the Pontine Marshes, encouraged mining, regulated fisheries, instituted a postal service and reinvigorated the guilds (*collegia, scholae*) of artisans. His greatest achievement, however, was to give the country thirty years of internal peace.

Gold coin of Theodoric (493–526).

The mausoleum of Theodoric, Ravenna. The roof consists of a large monolith, 35 feet in diameter and weighing 470 tons.

Despite all these well-intentioned activities, Theodoric's ambition to weld Goths and Romans into a single Italian nation failed. The Goths remained a military caste, living under Gothic customary law administered by counts (*comites*). The direction of policy lay with the king and his council of Gothic notables. If the legal system of the empire was retained for the Romans, any clash of jurisdiction favoured the Goths. No Roman could bear arms, unless as a mercenary in the Gothic army. The ordinary professions and trades were in Roman hands, but these pursuits were despised by the military aristocracy.

Although like his fellow Goths an Arian, Theodoric's relations with the Church were at first amicable. However, in 523 Theodoric received an order from the emperor that all Arian churches in Italy were to be handed over to the Catholics. In retaliation Theodoric closed the Catholic churches. Thus by a single act he ranged against himself emperor, Pope and Roman people.

The closing years of Theodoric's reign were tragic; treachery, real or imagined, was met with acts of ferocious cruelty. When a charge of conspiracy with the Eastern court was brought against a Roman patrician, he was defended by Boëthius. Theodoric cast Boëthius into prison (where he wrote one of the most-read books in the Middle Ages, *De Consolatione Philosophiae*) and subsequently had him strangled (524). Boëthius' death aroused considerable sympathy, and the incensed Theodoric put to death without trial the philosopher's

Boëthius. From a medieval MS. of *De Consolatione Philosophiae*. The book was translated into English by King Alfred, and later by Chaucer.

Left: Amalsuntha, who acted as regent for her son Athalaric. *Right:* Gold coin depicting the Emperor Justinian.

father-in-law, the senator Symmachus. In 526 Theodoric died and was succeeded by his grandson, a minor, for whom his mother Amalsuntha, Theodoric's daughter, acted as regent, with Cassiodorus as first minister.

Dissensions which arose among the Gothic nobles brought about the banishment and murder of Amalsuntha (533), and her death served the Emperor Justinian (527–65) as a *casus belli* for the recovery of Italy, an object which he had long contemplated. Justinian was fortunate in his generals, Belisarius and the eunuch Narses, and the protracted Gothic war (535–53) ended in a complete imperialist victory, which spelt the collapse of Gothic domination in Italy. During the war the senate, an institution of more than a thousand years, disappeared, the majority of its members, held as hostages by the Goths, being massacred. The devastation of the cities and countryside after almost twenty years of warfare and invasion was incalculable: Rome itself changed hands five times; whole regions remained desolate and depopulated, and famine was followed by outbreaks of plague. The substitution of corrupt Byzantine officials and grasping tax-collectors for the Gothic overlords gave no redress to the desperate condition of the surviving inhabitants. Italy was virtually under martial law, since generals were appointed by the Byzantine commander Narses, to be responsible only to him, as prefects of administrative districts known as 'duchies'.

17

From the *Life of St Benedict*
by Pope Gregory the Great.
Codex in the Vatican.

The period in which Justinian was attempting to assert his temporal and spiritual supremacy over the inhabitants of Italy was noteworthy for two events of major importance in the history of Western Europe. Although there had been earlier attempts to transplant Eastern monastic rules, the true founder of Western monasticism was Saint Benedict of Nursia (Norcia, 480–c. 543), who established a group of twelve monasteries near Subiaco. Becoming disgusted with the dissoluteness of the monks, he made his way south and at Monte Cassino built the monastery (529) which for centuries was looked on as the most important in Christendom. The Rule which he gave his Benedictines formed the pattern for later-founded Orders; it included the necessity of manual labour, with the result that his monasteries and those of subsequent foundation, such as Bobbio, Farfa, Nonantola, Santa Giulia di Brescia and Cava de' Tirreni, with their daughter communities, became models of estate management.

The second event which distinguished the reign of Justinian was the vast compilation of Roman law undertaken at the emperor's command by a com-

Illuminated MS. from the Vatican Library. St Benedict, the founder of the Abbey of Monte Cassino, with the Abbot Desiderius (1059–86, Pope Victor III, 1086–7), who rebuilt the Abbey and founded a school of Byzantine-influenced mosaicists and painters whose work spread through much of southern Italy. Examples are the beautiful murals at S. Maria in Formis near Capua.

mission headed by the jurist Tribonian in the years 528–34. The three principal books of the *Corpus Juris* were indispensable for the study and practice of Roman law, and remain to this day its authoritative source.

Among the barbarian mercenaries employed by Narses against the Goths was a contingent of Lombards (*Langobardi*, *Longobardi*, Long-beards), under the chieftain Audoin. These troops behaved with such savagery that Narses was obliged to repatriate them to their territories on the Danube. Earlier the Lombards had migrated from farther north, possibly from Scandinavia. Now, pressed from the north by the Avars, in 568 Audoin's son, Alboin, judging accurately the defenceless state of Italy under the Byzantines, led the Lombard nation, with elements of other tribes (including a body of Saxons), over the Julian Alps, and within eighteen months most of northern and central Italy was in their possession. Italy appeared to lie at the mercy of these most barbaric of her barbarian conquerors.

PRAE SUL GREGORIUS
SEP TENO PNEUMATE
PLE NUS
OBS CURU VATEM DILU
CIDAT EZE CHIELEM
CAE SAR CA RE DO
NANTER SUS
PE
HOC MODI
MUN QUOD DA
BI PAUP AMI CUS
PECTORIS INCERO

Chapter Two

POPES AND EMPERORS, 568–1122

From the outset the Lombard domination showed a fissiparous tendency, an inability to consolidate the territories overrun into a unified Italic kingdom. Bands of barbarians, united seemingly on a clanship basis (*fare*), acting independently, set up 'duchies' in those Roman *civitates* they occupied. After the murders of the first two kings, Alboin and Cleph, no further election was held for ten years (574–84); in the prevailing anarchy the dukes – there were some thirty-five of them – sought to retain or extend the possessions they had seized. Each Lombard warrior (*arimanno, exercitalis*) became a landowner, replacing the dispossessed Romans and Goths. The dukes took over the former crown lands for themselves, the vast estates of the Church suffering partition in the same way as public and private property.

Attacks from the Byzantines and the Franks (the latter encouraged by subsidies from the Emperor Maurice) led to the necessity of providing some central authority and Authari was elected king in 584. To provide for a royal demesne, the dukes surrendered half their estates, which were thenceforth administered by officials known as *gastaldi*. In common with the later feudal practice in northern Europe, the Lombard kings raised and maintained a following of armed men, *gasindi*, to whom they granted fiefs.

Even if they had achieved political cohesion the Lombards were perhaps too few to occupy by force of arms the whole peninsula. Moreover, they possessed no fleet and controlled no major ports, except Genoa and Pisa, which they allowed to decay: the Byzantines, by means of their navy, could be reinforced and revictualled from the sea. Hence followed the Lombard-Byzantine territorial dualism, with its enduring political and social consequences. The Lombard state consisted in the north of the regions we now know as

◄ Pope Gregory the Great and the Emperor Henry II. From an early eleventh-century illuminated MS.

Piedmont, Lombardy, Emilia and northern Venezia; south of the Apennines were the duchies of Tuscia (Tuscany), Spoleto and Benevento. Byzantine Italy, nominally under a governor-general (*exarch*) at Ravenna but steadily becoming fragmented into virtually independent cities and territories, also under dukes, consisted of Istria; maritime Venice; Ravenna and its hinterland, which included Bologna and Ferrara (the 'exarchate' in the usual, restricted sense); the 'pentapolis' (Rimini, Pesaro, Fano, Sinigaglia and Ancona); the duchy of

Façade of the palace of the Byzantine Exarchs, Ravenna. Sixth century.

Rome, extending from Civitavecchia to Gaeta; Naples and its territory; Amalfi; both the 'heel' and 'toe' of Italy, with the important ports of Bari, Brindisi, Otranto, Gallipoli, Taranto and Reggio; and the islands of Sicily, Sardinia and Corsica.

In the year of Authari's death (590) the clergy and people of Rome elected as their bishop the man who was to secure the pre-eminence of the bishops of Rome over the four Eastern patriarchs and to lay the foundations of the medieval papacy. Gregory I (590–604) transformed the traditional respect which was owed to the occupant of the throne of St Peter into an authority so complete that, although it might afterwards be dimmed, it was never extinguished. His character and abilities were peculiarly Roman; an antique cast of mind was tempered by the fervour of his Christian faith. He first entered on a political career, where his birth, riches and practical intelligence led to his early appoint-ment as prefect of Rome. At thirty-six, forsaking politics, he was ordained deacon. After some years spent as a monk, occupied chiefly in theological exegesis, he was employed by the bishop of Rome, Pelagius II (578–90), as his nuncio in Constantinople. On the latter's death, so widely recognized were Gregory's moral and intellectual powers that he was unanimously elected to the vacant see.

The tasks that faced him were formidable. Rome was stricken with the plague. The Lombards had confiscated the estates of the Church in northern and central Italy, and under King Agilulf were threatening Rome itself. The Eastern emperor was powerless to furnish aid, while the exarch was virtually a prisoner in Ravenna. Yet by vigorous defensive measures and patient diplo-macy Gregory saved Rome. So multifarious were his concerns that, as he him-self confessed, 'he did not know if his office was that of a pastor or a temporal prince'. His correspondence was enormous; everywhere he exhorted bishops and cities to resist the barbarian heretics, the 'unspeakable Lombard race' – *gens nefandissima Langobardorum*. He rebuked the emperor for the extortions of Byzantine officials, poured scorn on the pretensions of the patriarch of Constanti-nople, reasoned with the Lombard king and the dukes, supported the bishops in Spain and Africa against heretics, and entered into friendly relations with the Catholic Queen Theodolinda with a view to the conversion of the Lombards. The municipal government of Rome was in his hands; and he set to work to rescue the patrimony of the Church and to superintend the detailed administra-tion of its estates, with the result that on his death the papacy was the first financial power of the time.

Everywhere his presence was felt. The reform of the ritual of the Mass and the development of church music (the Gregorian plainsong) were his contributions to the Church's liturgical and aesthetic riches. Of Gregory's manifold activities perhaps those that redounded most to the power and prestige of the papacy were the use he made of the growing monastic movement and the conversion of England in 596. He brought under his personal care the Benedictine foundations, granting them privileges and exemptions from episcopal jurisdiction, so that there were in every part of Europe bodies of men dedicated directly to the papacy. When, 120 years after St Augustine's landing in England, the Englishman St Boniface set out (716) to evangelize the Saxons, the Churches of England and Germany henceforth increasingly looked to the Popes not as bishops of Rome but as the Vicars of Christ on earth. Thus, when the time came for the Popes to give a lead in severing relations with Constantinople, freeing Italy from Lombard domination, and restoring the Roman empire of the West, it was on the basis of a reinvigorated and authoritative Church, whose institutions owed much to the doctrine and practice of Gregory the Great.

Panel of ivory antiphonary in the Fitzwilliam Museum, Cambridge, showing a bishop blessing. Ninth-tenth century.

The Iconoclastic controversy: partisans and their adversaries. From an eleventh-century psalter.

The Eastern emperors had always considered it within the imperial competence to decide on matters of Christian doctrine and to ratify the election of Popes. In the East theological disputes almost invariably assumed a political colouring, which often resulted in revolts and insurrections, so that there the ecclesiastical policy of the emperors (*caesaropapalism*) was perhaps politically justified. On the refusal of Pope Martin I (649–51) to accept the Emperor Constans' ruling in the controversy over the 'double nature' of Christ, he was arrested by the exarch, deported to Constantinople and imprisoned in the Crimea, where he died.

The events which brought about the final separation of East and West were also in a measure theological. A strong emperor, Leo the Isaurian (718–41), hard pressed in the defence of his dominions against the armies of Islam, found it necessary to increase taxation throughout the empire. At the same time, to avoid internal dissension and promote doctrinal and political uniformity, he published an edict (726) ordering all religious images in churches to be destroyed or removed. The result was very different from his intention. Revolts arose in the East which had to be suppressed by military force; in the West Pope Gregory II (715–31) withheld the increased taxes and the people rose in defence of their sacred images. In Rome, Naples, Venice, Ravenna and other cities of the exarchate, dukes were appointed independent of Constantinople in all but name. The breach was widened when a council called by Pope Gregory III in 731 excommunicated the iconoclasts, including the emperor.

In the year 629 Mahomet captured Mecca. Within eighty years of the Prophet's death in 632 the Moslem armies were victorious from the Indian to the Atlantic Oceans. Cyprus fell to them in 649; then their armies, in conjunction with their newly constructed fleets, took the diocese of Africa from the Byzantines. Crossing into Spain, the eastern Moslems (Saracens) in alliance with the converted Berbers of North Africa defeated the Visigoths (711) and established their ascendancy in the Iberian peninsula. The importance of the defeat of the Moslem army between Tours and Poitiers by the Franks under Charles Martel (732) has perhaps been exaggerated, since the impetus of the Moslem invasion was already slackening from internal causes. Nevertheless, the presence of the Moslems as the dominant sea-power in the Mediterranean for two hundred years was a serious blow to the West, and particularly to Italy.

The long reign of Liutprand (712–44) marked the high tide of Lombard civilization; an orthodox Catholic, he built monasteries and churches, and favoured Roman influences. Yet he was spurred on to extend the Lombard kingdom and to bring to heel the too independent dukes of Spoleto and Benevento, whom Gregory III was playing off against him. Threatened by

The Iron Crown of Lombardy, now in the treasury of Monza Cathedral. Napoleon crowned himself with this crown.

Late reliquary bust of the
Emperor Charlemagne, *c.* 1350.

Liutprand, Gregory appealed in vain for assistance from Charles Martel, the
mayor of the palace to the Frankish king. Finally, when in 752 Liutprand's
successor, King Astulf, captured Ravenna, Pope Stephen II (752–57) crossed
the Alps, crowned Pipin king of the Franks (thus confirming the deposition of
the Merovingian *rois fainéants*), and obtained from him in return a promise to
invade Italy and 'restore the exarchate and all other places and rights belonging
to the republic of Rome'. Pipin fulfilled his promise, defeating Astulf and
demanding that the liberated cities of the exarchate and the pentapolis be
handed over not to the 'republic of Rome' but to 'St Peter' (756). On the Lombards' failure to honour the terms of their undertaking to do this, Pipin's successor, his son Charles, crossed the Alps, captured Pavia, the Lombard capital,
and deposed the last of their kings, Desiderius (774).

Charlemagne (as Charles become known in his lifetime, in recognition of his
greatness) now added to his Frankish kingdom that of the Lombards. About
the time of Stephen's visit to Pipin there had appeared a document known as the

*Carolingian
Revival*

St Peter with Pope Leo III
and the Emperor Charlemagne.
From a watercolour by
Grimaldi, after a ninth-century
mosaic in the church of S.
Giovanni in Laterano, Rome.
Now in the Vatican Library.

Donation of Constantine, a pious forgery possibly emanating from the papal chancery. It purported to be a fourth-century deed, whereby the Emperor Constantine conferred on Bishop Silvester the city of Rome and all the towns and provinces of Italy and of the West, 'because it is not right that the secular emperor should have authority where the principality of priests and the head of the Christian religion was established by the Heavenly Emperor'. It is not known in entirety what provisions the *Donation of Pipin* contained, but certainly the cession of the exarchate and the pentapolis constituted the quasi-juridical foundation of the Papal States. Charlemagne confirmed his father's donation, issuing a fresh document, although its contents are disputed; as protector of the Church and king of the Lombards, however, he undoubtedly assumed his sovereignty over Italy, even if his actual power hardly reached far south of Rome, where Lombards and Byzantines were in effective possession. The coronation of Charlemagne as Emperor Augustus by Pope Leo III on Christmas Day 800, thus restoring (or re-creating) the Roman empire of the

The clerical hierarchy.
Miniature from an exultet
roll, formerly in the
monastery of S. Vincenzo al
Volturno, now in the
Vatican Library.

West, was in an important sense only a supererogatory papal sanction to an established political fact. Charlemagne, by right of inheritance and of conquest, had extended his territorial sovereignty over an area stretching from the North Sea to the Ebro and to Benevento, from the Atlantic to the Elbe and the Danube. In this politico-religious act of papal investiture lay the seeds of future conflict between the Empire and the papacy for supremacy over Western Christendom.

Charlemagne governed his Italian kingdom, as the other divisions of his vast empire, through the agency of counts, who combined both judicial and military powers. But for the first thirty years he left the government of the counties to Lombard counts and officials, only gradually replacing them by Franks. In accordance with his thoroughly theocratic ideas of the relation of State and Church, he associated the bishops with the counts. He used the hierarchy of the Church as his bureaucracy, guiding the administration of the most distant parts by the issue of edicts, or capitularies; and he kept control over local activities by means of imperial envoys (*missi dominici*), whose duty was to

29

The Emperor
Charles 'the Bald'.

check abuses and to report directly to him. With the Englishman Alcuin as his chief adviser, he worked for the achievement of this theocratic ideal, based on the spiritual and temporal natures of man. As might have been foreseen, the harmonious relation of Pope and Emperor in strict accordance with the so-called Gelasian theory of the two powers, the wielders, in contemporary language, of the spiritual and temporal swords, was dependent primarily on the personality of the Emperor; and it did not outlive Charlemagne.

The partition of the Carolingian Empire after Charlemagne's death in 814, with the possessor of Italy enjoying only a nominal ascendancy with the title of Emperor, was favourable at first to the papacy. Nicholas I (858–67) was not without success in claiming the superiority of the pontifical power, using for this purpose the *pseudo-Isidorian Decretals*, a series of forged documents which asserted among other things the supremacy of the papacy over the whole body of the episcopate. Pope John VIII (872–82) decided against the claims of the rightful heir to the Empire and crowned Charles the Bald in 875. The deposition of the last of the Carolingian Emperors, Charles the Fat, in 887, was followed by a period of feudal anarchy which has been perversely called by some Italian historians the era of the 'Independent Italic Kingdom'. In reality no one of the contestants could assert his authority over the whole country, which was rent with the struggle between the dukes of Spoleto and Friuli (among other claimants), who forced the Popes to crown them; and in the general degradation the papacy was relegated to being a mere perquisite of the *de facto* possessor of Rome. The activities of Theodora and her daughter Marozia about the papal throne and the papal bed read like some *chronique scandaleuse*. For years the papacy was treated as a temporal fief, disputed between Roman factions headed by the families of Tusculum and Crescentius. Alberich, Marozia's son, imprisoned his mother; and, ruling Rome as *princeps* and senator (932–54), forced the nobles on oath to accept as his successor and Pope his son John XII (955–63), a youth of sixteen. It was not until the mid-eleventh century that a succession of German Popes was to inaugurate a period of reform, inspired by the ideals of Cluny.

As early as the beginning of the ninth century, in the lifetime of Charlemagne, the coasts of Italy and the islands were subject to constant raids from the Moslems of Spain and Africa. The conquest of Sicily by the Aghlabid dynasty of Africa began in 827; Palermo fell in 831 and Messina in 843. But it was not until 878 that Syracuse was captured, and it took until 902, with the destruction of Taormina, for Moslem rule to be established throughout Sicily.

Well before this time the Moslems were in southern Italy, intervening on one side or the other in the wars between Naples and the Lombard rulers of Benevento, Salerno and Capua. We hear of Moslems in Naples in 837. Byzantine Italy proved for them an easy prey; Taranto was taken, and a few years later (841?) Bari, which was to remain their main base of operation for thirty years, until it was recaptured by the Emperor Louis VI. In August 846 a strong Moslem fleet appeared off Ostia; in the attack on Rome which followed, the churches of St Peter's and St Paul-without-the-Walls were desecrated, and the Borgo (Trastevere) laid waste. It was after this event that Pope Leo IV (847–55) enclosed the Borgo with walls – the 'Leonine City'. Three years later a papal fleet, with a strong contingent from Naples, Gaeta and Amalfi, inflicted a severe defeat on the Moslems off Ostia. Yet some time after 878 the Moslems were able to establish a permanent foothold on the River Garigliano, from which they raided up to the gates of Rome. In 888 they destroyed the abbey of Monte Cassino. It required the combined forces of 'King' Berengar, Pope John X and the Byzantines finally to destroy their camp in 915.

It was not until the coming of the Normans in the eleventh century that the Moslems in Sicily and southern Italy were finally overpowered; yet the corsairs of North Africa remained a menace as late as the early nineteenth century. Further to add to the misery of the inhabitants of Italy, there first appeared at the end of the ninth century marauding bands of savage Magyar horsemen (related ethnically to the Huns), who carried their devastating raids deep into southern Italy. These invasions were only terminated with the Magyar defeat at Lechfeld in 955 by the Germans under the Saxon king, later the Emperor Otto I (962–73).

Nevertheless, these centuries in which Italy, riven by internal dissension, lay apparently defenceless against any external attack, a period which from the unrelieved misery and destruction suffered by the Italian peoples merits the name of the 'Dark Ages', saw a revival salutary for the future. The people were forced to look to their own defence: the walls of cities and towns were built or repaired, bourgs were constructed under the protection of the feudal castles, and above all those men capable of bearing arms were trained in their use. With the Carolingian Emperors and their successors a new Frankish-Germanic nobility had grown up beside, or supplanting, the Lombard nobles. If it has been said that the feudal system never really took root in Italy, this is a comparative statement. Certainly it did not show the developed features of French or German feudalism. It was a foreign graft that did not flourish on the native stock. Moreover, the system in Italy was to be overshadowed and defeated by what is one of the glories of Italian history – the rise of the autonomous communes. Still, the existence of a numerous class of foreign (until the coming of the Spaniards, northern) feudatories, who battened on the productive classes in town and countryside and kept the peninsula in ferment with their quarrels and rivalries, was to be for centuries the bane of Italy.

In theory the count was the Emperor's official in the Italian *civitates* (the towns with their surrounding countryside); he together with the bishop, whose diocese usually corresponded with the 'county', carried on the administration in the Emperor's name. At first the counts were granted lands in precarious title; that is, they had the usufruct but not the possession. By a gradual process their estates became hereditary, a fact which was given imperial sanction by the capitulary of Kiersy (877). Besides these counts were nobles who possessed their lands in their own right; and further there were the great lords of the marches, such as the marquis of Ivrea, the marquis of Turin or the marquis of Friuli, who guarded the marches from the north-western to the north-eastern frontiers. Gradually, too, the domains of the crown were parcelled out in fiefs as rewards for service. The division of fiefs among the sons of the hereditary holders; the process of *commendation*, whereby a small landowner gave up his estate to a powerful lord, bishop or abbot and received it back *in beneficio*; and

Jesus predicts war and destruction. From a twelfth-century Byzantine gospel.

Ploughing scene from *Easter Sermon* of Gregory of Nazianzus. Eleventh century.

finally the practice of breaking up the fiefs into smaller fiefs – all these largely added to the great number of those holding lands in return for military service.

A distinction of importance in following the disintegration of Italian feudalism in face of the communes' opposition is that between *capitanei* (holders '*in capite*') and *vavasours*. In the first class were the greatest feudal dignitaries, the archbishops, bishops, those holding directly from the Emperor, the great allodial proprietors; all these together with their immediate vassals were known as *capitanei*. They in turn parcelled out their fiefs, also on a military basis, to subvassals, owing allegiance to their immediate lords. The sub-vassals and their arm-bearing dependants (who might also possess small fiefs) formed the class of vavasours (*valvassores*). These conditions held mostly in northern and central Italy; but in southern Italy also we hear of class divisions in the cities, where the free population was distinguished as *milites* or *cives*. The greatest landowners, or richest townsmen, were also known as *optimates*, and these would correspond with the northern *capitanei*, while the lesser *milites* formed the more numerous class of vavasours. It was the members of these two extensive classes, residing both in the cities and in their country castles, who by the eleventh century (when many Norman creations had swelled their ranks) were known as *nobles*.

In Italy the Emperors of the Franconian line sought to curb the great Italian nobles by supporting the vavasours, declaring them direct feudatories of the crown and not vassals or sub-vassals of their former lords. The period of the Saxon and Franconian Emperors (962–1125) coincided with an important stage in the development of municipal life, in which the powers of the bishops were increased at the expense of the counts. Somewhat earlier, in Modena in 892 and Bergamo in 904, the bishops had been given extensive jurisdiction within the city and its environs. In Parma in 962, and a few years later in Lodi, the bishop was granted all the former powers of the count. The result of these innovations was to separate the townsfolk from those who remained under the jurisdiction of the counts in the *contado* (the countryside, whence the designation *contadini*, countrymen or peasants). The completion of this process was when the bishop's civil jurisdiction extended over the whole diocese, as we find occurring in Vercelli in 999, in Parma in 1035 and in Bergamo in 1041.

Norman Conquest of South Italy   In southern Italy local animosities between the Lombard rulers of Benevento, Salerno and Capua, and their rivalry with Naples, all sides employing Moslem mercenaries, made petty warfare endemic. A revival of Byzantine power led

Left: Christ in mandorla, blessing the Emperor Henry III (1017–56) and his wife. From an illuminated MS of the *Gospels of Henry III*; mid-eleventh century. *Right:* Late twelfth-century miniature showing Pope Leo IX with the Abbot Warinus of St Arnulf.

to the formation of the 'theme of Lombardy', which comprised most of Apulia and was administered from Bari, first under a *strategos*, then from 975 under the 'Catapan of Italy'.

One of the romantic stories that tell of the coming of the Normans to the south of Italy relates how in 1017 a band of Norman pilgrims to the shrine of St Michael on Monte Gargano supported the Lombard Melo against the Byzantines. The first territorial foothold gained by these northern mercenaries was at Aversa, granted by the duke of Naples to Rainulf (1030) as a reward for his assistance against the Lombards of Capua. Among the leaders of these Norman bands, who intervened wherever their aid was sought, were the three elder sons of Tancred of Hauteville, William (*Braccio di Ferro*, Iron Arm), Drogo and Humphrey. William made himself count of Apulia, with his capital at Melfi, and his position was recognized by the Emperor Henry III in 1047. Of the twelve d'Hauteville brothers, or half-brothers, the most celebrated was Robert Guiscard (*guiscardo*, cunning); on the deaths of William, Drogo and Humphrey he was recognized as the Norman leader and later assumed the title of duke of Apulia and Calabria. In 1053 the troops of Pope Leo IX were routed by Robert Guiscard and Richard of Aversa, the Pope

35

Twelfth-century mosaic from the church of the Martorana, Palermo. Christ crowns King Roger the Norman as King of Sicily.

himself being taken prisoner. It would appear that his release after six months of captivity was effected by his recognition of the *fait accompli* of the Norman conquests, although it was Pope Nicholas II who invested Robert Guiscard with southern Italy and Sicily, when the latter should be conquered. With the capture of Bari in 1071 Byzantine power on the southern mainland was finally extinguished. Palermo fell to Robert's youngest brother Roger in 1072 and he proclaimed himself count under the overlordship of Duke Robert. Roger II, the son of the conqueror of Sicily, inherited the crown from his father in 1101, and added to his kingdom the Norman possessions on the mainland, thus being the effective founder of the kingdom of the Two Sicilies (1127), which he held not as the liegeman of either emperor but of the Pope (1130). The papacy saw in an alliance with the Normans a counterbalance to the German Emperors. Benevento became part of the Papal States, and remained in papal possession until the reunification of Italy.

When Cardinal Hildebrand was acclaimed Pope and took the name of Gregory VII (1073), he had already been the power behind the party dedicated to the reform of the Church since the time of Leo IX (1049). The reformers, originally inspired by the ideals of the Cluniac return to the purity of the earlier Benedictine Rule, had gained much support in Italy, where already two reformed Orders had been inaugurated – the Camaldolesi (1012) and the Vallombrosians (c. 1038). The reforming party had some strange allies among the poorer classes in Milan, the so-called *patarini*, who were violently opposed to the marriage ('concubinage') of the clergy. Another burning issue was that of simony, which in the course of time had altered its original meaning from the *sale* of ecclesiastical offices to that of any acceptance of investiture to religious office at the hands of a layman. This reform was naturally seen as directed particularly against the Emperor. In an attempt to break free from lay control, a Lateran Synod (1059) decreed that the election of Popes was thenceforth to be effected solely by the college of cardinals.

Cardinals leaving a conclave. From the *Richental Chronicle* in the Rosgartenmuseum, Constance.

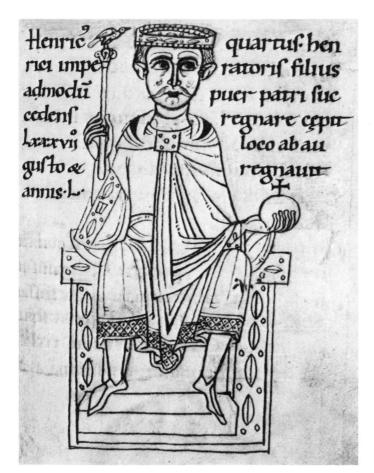

The Emperor Henry IV (1050–1106). From a miniature in the library of Corpus Christi College, Cambridge.

What was aimed at by the Hildebrandine party was nothing less than the complete supremacy of the papacy over the universal Church, with powers to appoint and dismiss bishops and the sole right to convoke general councils. Even some territorial sovereigns Gregory regarded as feudal vassals of the Holy See. His weapon was excommunication; and this he was not afraid to use against the Emperor Henry IV in 1076, leading to the latter's famous humiliation at the castle of Canossa (January 1077). Henry, however, later gained the upper hand, entered Rome and set up the anti-pope Clement III (1080). Gregory, shut in the Castel Sant'Angelo, called on his ally Robert Guiscard, who marched on Rome and, Henry and Clement having withdrawn, allowed his Normans to sack the city, with a fearful massacre of its inhabitants. Gregory accompanied Duke Robert to Salerno, where he died and was buried in the cathedral (25 May 1085). His last words were said to have been: 'I have loved justice and hated iniquity, and for this reason I die in exile.'

The War of Investitures between Popes and Emperors dragged on, until a settlement was reached in the Concordat of Worms (1122), a compromise whereby the Emperor renounced the investiture of bishops and abbots by the gift of the ring and pastoral staff (the religious investiture) but retained the right of investiture with the sceptre (the feudal investiture). The importance of this period for the history of Italy lay not so much in deciding these politico-religious matters, but that in the course of the struggle between Popes and Emperors we see the rise to maturity of the communes of northern and central Italy.

Pope Gregory VII, driven from Rome by the forces of Henry IV, was rescued by the Normans, and died in Salerno in May 1085. From the *Weltchronik* of Otto of Freising. Second half of the twelfth century.

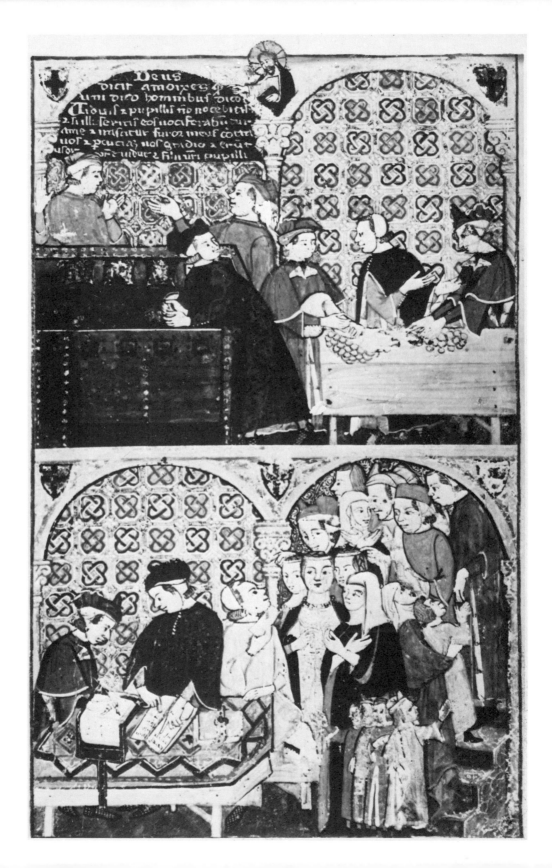

Chapter Three

THE COMMERCIAL REVOLUTION, *c.* 950–*c.* 1350

The period of four hundred years, roughly from the mid-tenth to the mid-fourteenth centuries, witnessed social changes of the deepest import to the history of the Italian peoples. Thenceforth Italy stood in the vanguard of European culture, until she was overwhelmed in the course of new barbarian invasions. The period saw the birth and growth of the autonomous communes. An efflorescence of social activities of all kinds marks the period as one of the most creative known to the West. In Italy as in Flanders, the other part of Europe which showed a comparable growth, the basis for this social advance was the same – namely, trade. Commerce led to industry, and the two activities in conjunction produced an accumulation of capital that allowed Italians to dominate European finance. On such a solid material foundation were achieved the splendours of the Renaissance.

In Lombard Italy, although there were regions where depopulation and devastation had brought about a relapse to a closed or natural economy based on the self-sufficiency of the manors (*villae, curtes*), in those parts which remained Byzantine, and these included most of the existing ports, a diminished but not nugatory trade was maintained with by far the richest European city, Constantinople. By the eighth century the existence of mints in a number of cities suggests the rapid extension of an exchange economy. At about this time we hear of the existence of free merchants (*negotiatores*): King Liutprand granted (715) to the merchants of Comacchio special privileges with regard to payment of tolls on the River Po. Similarly, documents refer now to urban markets and town-dwelling artisans. Of especial interest are the *magistri commacini*; whether this name is derived from the town of Como or from *cum machina* (i.e. scaffolding) is disputed, but there is no doubt that it refers to those bodies of itinerant masons

41

and builders to whom we owe the magnificent solidity and vigorous plasticity of so much Romanesque building.

In the correspondence of Gregory the Great, during the chaos of the Lombard invasion, we find references to the annual sailings of ships from the ports of Rome (Ostia), Ravenna and Naples bound for the islands, Provence, Africa and the East. The Moslem market, moreover, was immense, extending from China and India to the Atlantic. Italy now found herself admirably placed as a centre of distribution between Catholic Europe, the Byzantine East and the Moslem world. Politically as well, her position gave her advantages which she was quick to exploit. Venice, Naples, Bari, Amalfi, Gaeta and other ports were still, at least officially, subject to Constantinople and had access to the markets of the Eastern capital; their Lombard-Frankish-Germanic hinterland provided sources of supply as well as increasingly receptive markets.

Even in the ninth century Amalfi, Naples and Gaeta were trading with the Moslems of Sicily and Africa, and with Greeks, Syrians and Jews, who thronged their markets. Pisa, too, traded with Sardinia and Corsica, and indulged in some profitable piracy; and early in the eleventh century Genoa joined in the increasing maritime activity in the Tyrrhenian Sea. The smuggling of slaves to the East or to Moslem Spain was a lucrative business; there was a 'manufactory' of eunuchs on the island of Favignana off western Sicily. Besides slaves, timber, raw iron and iron goods, Italy was beginning to export textiles. Salt, too, was a commodity much in demand and was produced by Pisa, Comacchio and above all Venice; the last-named had also a trade with Constantinople in salted fish. The earliest imports into Italy that the documents record were spices (particularly pepper), scents, ivory, olive oil and rare textiles such as silk. Later Venice imported corn, at first for herself, then for re-export. The basis of the rapidly increasing wealth of these Italian cities was found in their functions as entrepôts and carriers; they were first intermediaries rather than producers.

In about 1000 Venice, by virtue of her business acumen, naval prowess and highly developed diplomacy, had achieved a commanding position as the great trading link between Europe and the East. Though nominally Byzantine, her doges negotiated as equals with Emperors, Popes, kings, caliphs and cities, securing privileges in the form of markets, monopolies and reductions in excise duties – such negotiations led to the *pactum* of 840 with the Emperor Lothair, and the famous Golden Bull (992) with the Byzantine emperor. In Constantinople and other Eastern cities Venetian merchants had their own quarters

Left: Masons at work. From a Byzantine psalter miniature.

Right: Portrait of the Emperor Lothair (d. 855).

Trade with the East: Eastern merchants and ship. From a codex of Aristotle's *Ethics*.

under their own officials. Agreements with the towns of northern Italy gave Venetian traders access to their markets and to the passes over the Alps to Germany and the Low Countries. The ports of Istria and several Dalmatian towns and islands, which Venice cleared of pirates, were forced to accept her suzerainty. As in Constantinople, Venice had her state-controlled compounds (*xenodochia*) for the accommodation of foreign merchants visiting the city, as well as warehouses (*fondachi*) for their goods.

The widening of this market economy in the sea coast towns hastened the decline of the manorial system, the lords' demesnes becoming increasingly farmed on leasehold (*emphyteusis* and *libelli*), with stipulations as to improvements – the clearing of woodland and marsh, and the planting of vines, olives and orchards. Sometimes more advanced works were initiated – flood-control, drainage and even irrigation. By the tenth century Italy was on the way to redressing centuries of regression and to becoming again the garden of Europe.

Page from an Arabic translation of Galen, with 'portraits' of famous ancient physicians.

The debt of the Italians to the Moslem world in respect of commercial and technical (including agricultural) innovations has not always been adequately recognized. The Moslems had early developed a banking system, receiving deposits, discounting bills, dealing in foreign exchange, granting loans and farming taxes. But perhaps their greatest contribution was in the transmission of the Hindu numerals (wrongly, but understandably, called 'Arabic') to the West. Mathematics must have made great strides by the time Leonardo of Pisa published his great work, the *Liber Abaci*, in 1202. (Double-entry book-keeping, however, was an Italian invention of the fourteenth century.) The Arabs brought sugar-cane, cotton, citrus fruits and rice to Sicily; from the Chinese they learned the production of silk and paper; and from them also they adopted the use of the magnetic compass. Until the eleventh century the bulk of Mediterranean trade in luxuries was in Moslem hands: a list of such articles glows like a description from *The Arabian Nights*.

Medieval medical practice. From a treatise translated from the Latin of Roger of Salerno (fl. 1180).

Chinese mariner's compass. Date uncertain, but the Chinese anticipated the Italians in the use of the lodestone for navigational purposes.

Commercial Revolution Then in the course of the eleventh century the tide of Moslem commercial ascendancy was reversed in favour of Italy. By the twelfth century Venice, Genoa, Pisa and the greater or smaller coastal cities, with those of their hinter-land, gained an economic primacy which was maintained with a growing momentum until the chaos following the Black Death closed the era of the 'Commercial Revolution' in the mid-fourteenth century. For Italy this was a golden age, which already in many fields of activity heralded the achievements of the Renaissance. The nascent bourgeoisie broke the feudal trammels, brought liberty to the serfs (but not a share in the government), and turned itself, to-gether with those elements of the nobility which it had absorbed, into a new aristocracy of wealth. And it used its money well: hospitals, asylums, alms-houses, schools and universities were founded and endowed; there was a burgeoning of architecture, art and literature unseen since classical times; a revival in liberal studies, in science and law; and a new consciousness of the spiritual and intellectual possibilities of men which was in complete contrast with the Dark Ages. This bourgeois revolution in Italy, based unashamedly on commerce and industry and flying in the face of ecclesiastical strictures against such practices as usury or dealing in futures (summed up in the sin of Avarice), has been seen as one of the great turning-points in history and the seedbed of much that is characteristic of our own contemporary civilization.

Italian merchants, journeying north over the Alpine passes, had as early as the twelfth century penetrated the Flemish and English wool markets and were familiar figures at the fairs of Champagne. Fine cloths began to be exported by the Italians to Africa and the East to pay for luxuries, and also in exchange for the necessary dyestuffs and alum, which were required for the cloth industry both in northern Europe and now increasingly in the cities of north and central Italy. A list of tariffs at Venice for the year 1265 shows over thirty different English or Flemish cloths, but only some ten Italian kinds. This state of affairs

The Fourth Crusade, 1204. The surrender of Constantinople. ▶
From a pavement mosaic in the church of S. Giovanni Evangelistica, Rome.

was rapidly changed. Industry became combined with commerce. Italian towns bought the coarse northern cloths and became expert in the processes of dyeing and finishing. In Florence by the middle of the twelfth century the merchants of the finishing industry had constituted themselves into a guild, the Arte di Calimala, and they were soon followed by the Arte della Lana, which dealt with the whole process of cloth-making and ultimately outstripped its older rival, producing annually some 100,000 pieces of cloth. Throughout the Po region, in Venetia and Tuscany the woollen industry became the principal source of commercial and industrial prosperity. Lucca was the earliest city to win fame for its silks; Cremona produced fustian; but by the early fourteenth century all these cities had yielded pride of place, in manufacture of fine cloths, to Florence.

The large capital sums accumulated by Italian businessmen were employed in the most varied activities of a speculative nature; there was a diaspora of Italians in search of gain throughout the cities of Europe, Africa and the East. While northern chivalry shed its blood in futile crusades, the Italians (particularly the Venetians, Pisans and Genoese) turned political events to their own commercial gain. In the first three crusades (1095–99, 1147–49, 1189–92) all three cities played a part; but in the fourth crusade, which set up the Latin empire in Constantinople in 1204, it was Venice that reaped the huge profits of success.

Then in 1261 Genoa aided the Byzantine emperor in retaking Constantinople and replaced Venice for a short time in exploiting the Eastern trade. On the shores of the Black Sea were the sites of flourishing Venetian and Genoese colonies, which dealt in furs, leather and fish from Russia, as well as Oriental goods from as far afield as China and India. Where the Polos had led, other merchants followed, so that when in the early fourteenth century the Florentine Francesco Pegolotti wrote his celebrated commercial manual, the *Practica della mercatura*, he took it for granted that merchants required knowledge of Chinese mercantile practice. The customs dues in the harbour of Genoa increased fourfold between 1274 and 1293, in the latter year producing 3,822,000 lire (in Genoese currency), an income seven times in excess of that of the French king. The dues from the colonies roughly equalled those of the mother city. Before the close of the thirteenth century annual convoys of Venetian and Geno-ese galleys were seen in the Atlantic on visits to the ports of Flanders and

Left: King Edward III of England.

Right: The Florentine florin, and *(below)* the Venetian ducat.

England. By the early fourteenth century the main cities of Italy surpassed in population all those of Western Europe, with the exception of Paris.

Italian businessmen in England, France and Flanders in the late twelfth century came mostly from Milan, Cremona, Asti and Piacenza (even the little town of Chieri was known in the Low Countries for its pawnbrokers); subsequently the Sienese, Lucchese, Pistoians and especially the Florentines were the most prominent. Only later did Genoese bankers enter the international markets. The brothers 'Mouche' and 'Biche' Guidi of the Florentine firm of Frescobaldi and Franzoni were financial advisers to Philip the Fair of France. Similarly in England the Italian houses of Ricardi, Frescobaldi (the head of the London branch was a member of Edward II's council), Bardi and Peruzzi acted as papal representatives and speculated particularly in the export of fine wools. Edward III defaulted in his debt of 1,365,000 florins to the Florentine banking companies of Bardi and Peruzzi, bringing them to bankruptcy (1338). The minting of the gold Florentine florin in 1252, which was followed presently by the Venetian ducat, greatly facilitated exchange, since they were universally accepted.

During the eleventh century the cities in northern and central Italy began to make strides towards full municipal freedom. In the forefront was Milan. In 1018 Aribert was appointed archbishop, and so extended his power in Lombardy that Milanese ambitions provoked the bitter hostility of the citizens of

Formation of the Communes

◀ Marco Polo (*c.* 1254–1324) departing from Venice. From a fourteenth-century MS. in the Bodleian Library, Oxford.

Pavia, Lodi, Como and Cremona. Warfare, which had broken out in Milan between *capitanei* (supported by the *cives*, i.e. merchants, justices, notaries – the nascent bourgeoisie) and vavasours, spread to other parts of Lombardy, and Aribert, who favoured his own class of *capitanei*, called on the Emperor Conrad II (1027–39) for assistance. Conrad unexpectedly sided with the vavasours (*Constitutio de feudis* 1037). The Emperor's efforts to subdue the rebellious Milanese with the aid of Pavia and Lodi were unsuccessful, and events in Germany ultimately caused his withdrawal north of the Alps. (To Archbishop Aribert incidentally is owed the peculiar construction known as the *carroccio*, which was copied by other Italian cities: this was a waggon drawn by oxen, bearing an altar and the city's banner; it served as the army's rallying-point.)

A step in the emancipation of Milan from archiepiscopal rule now followed. When a vavasour ill-treated a burgher, the people drove the nobles, with Archbishop Aribert, from the city: they had proved themselves capable of withstanding both the Emperor and their own nobility. Thenceforth the government of the city passed from the archbishop to the freemen, whether *capitanei*, vavasours or rich burghers, who exercised 'in common' (*comune*) the former feudal rights and powers, military, civil and fiscal. A new constitution was ratified by the Emperor Henry III in 1055, and from this year we may date the birth of the Milanese commune.

By the end of the fourteenth century practically all the towns of northern and central Italy found they could exploit the Wars of the Investitures to their own advantage and had achieved civic autonomy. In the south a similar tendency was halted by King Roger II, and such municipal liberties as existed were abolished by the Emperor Frederick II. The types of communal constitutions (or rather those of the 'city-states', since the cities, with their class of resident landowning nobles, found themselves in possession of much of the surrounding countryside) were not universally identical, but showed a strong family likeness. They were invariably oligarchies; only the nobility and the rich (*popolo grasso*) shared in the government. At the head of the *comune civitatis*, as the city's administration became known, were consuls, varying in number and duration of office. We hear of them in Lucca, Pisa and Pavia in about 1084, in Milan in 1097, in Como in 1109, in Bologna in 1123 and in Piacenza in 1126. They were assisted by an elected privy council, known usually as the *credenza*. Below this council was a larger elected body, numbering some hundreds, and called variously the *gran consiglio* (grand council), senate, or council of the commune. Finally there was the meeting of the free burghers in their *parlamento* (also termed *arengo* or

Medieval towers in Bologna. In the foreground, the Torre Asinelli (1109, height 225 feet); behind it, the Torre Garisenda (1100, height 130 feet).

concione), but they had no power of debate, merely accepting or rejecting pro-posals put to them by the councils.

As the power of the guilds grew, they gained an important voice in matters of state, especially the greater guilds of the wool-dealers, merchants and bankers. These mercantile corporations were not the only associations; as the influence of the commune spread over the whole of the former diocese, the remaining feudal nobles were overcome and forced to live within the city for at least some months of the year. We find them joining with the city nobility in associations called *consorterie*, often grouped together in a district. Here they raised those defensive towers, which we can still see in Bologna, Mantua and the little town of San Gimignano, and laid out their covered meeting-places (*loggie*) in the squares. *Una famiglia di torre e loggia* became an expression for a noble family. Lastly, the city was divided into wards, each under a military leader, for pur-poses of attack and defence.

Warfare between cities was only too frequent; it is a matter of surprise that such achievement of material growth should have been accompanied by almost incessant armed hostility. As a rule it may be said that neighbouring cities tended to be hostile, wars arising from disputed territory (in north and central Italy the average distance from one commune to another was only twenty to twenty-five miles), desire to control the main trade routes (passes, roads, rivers), or simply from motives of security; and leagues tended to be formed with other cities adjoining the main adversary. Thus Milan, the old Roman capital, and its neighbour Pavia, the Teutonic capital, were natural opponents. Bologna and Modena were also frequently at variance, the first finding support from Reggio and Ferrara, while Modena allied herself with Parma and Cremona. In the Veneto Padua, Vicenza and Verona grew in importance and were constantly in opposition to each other. To the east of Treviso feudal lords held sway. In Tuscany the struggles lay principally between Florence, Pisa, Lucca and Siena.

Florentines attacking Pistoia. Illustration from Villani's *Cronache* in the Vatican Library, showing a *carroccio* and the flags of Venice and of Pistoia. Fourteenth century.

Ghibelline seal.   Guelf seal.

The terms Guelf and Ghibelline (Italianized forms of German Welf and Waiblingen, the family names of rival claimants to the Empire) came to be used as party catchwords in Italy towards the middle of the thirteenth century. In general they were employed to designate the supporters of Popes and Emperors respectively, but they had no invariably fixed connotation; they served only to discriminate between leagues and parties engaged in hostilities, and these would often vary bewilderingly with changes in circumstances. Some cities were predominantly Guelf (e.g. Florence, Milan and Bologna) or Ghibelline (Cremona, Pavia and Pisa); but even within these we find the terms employed by opposing factions.

Venice

The constitution of Venice, one of the earliest of the autonomous oligarchies, was in many respects peculiar. In 813 the seat of the government of the confederated islands of the lagoons was transferred to the Rivoalto (Rialto). Doges had been elected by the islanders at least as early as 697. In 1032 a law was passed in the *arengo*, appointing a privy council (the *consiglieri ducali*) and a senate, the *pregadi* (the 'invited'), to limit the doge's powers. From the beginning a merchant aristocracy developed, until it ultimately formed a closed oligarchy. In 1171 a council of 480 members was set up, which became in time the *gran consiglio*. The formation of a body to investigate the late doge's proceedings (1198) strengthened the aristocracy's preponderance in all affairs of state. The closing (*serratura*) of the *gran consiglio* to new families, a measure of 1296, put the seal on the Venetian oligarchy; and the creation of the notorious council of ten (made permanent in 1335) made any attempt at change, democratic or otherwise, a hazardous undertaking.

The Emperor Henry IV asks the Countess Matilda of Tuscany and Abbot Hugh of Cluny to intercede on his behalf with Pope Gregory VII, *c.* 1076.

Florence   In the history of the origins of the Italian communes one of the most famous, Florence, was a late starter. Only in the time of the Countess Matilda, the last of the German house of the marquises of Tuscany (although Florence was already on its way to commercial and industrial prosperity), do we find signs of nascent communal activity. During the countess's absence – the capital of the marquisate was Lucca – Florence was administered by a body of officials known as the 'good men' (*boni homines*), who, on the death of the countess (1115) and the bequest of her territories to the papacy, took over the government in the name of the people. In 1138 we find these officials' titles changed to consuls – there appear to have been twelve, chosen by the nobility (*grandi* or *delle torri*) and assisted by a council of a hundred in which the guilds (*arti*) were prominent. Dissensions within the city led to the appointment of a foreign head of state, the *podestà*; and a *consiglio del comune* was set up alongside the older council.

In 1249 the Ghibelline nobles drove into exile their Guelfic rivals, but in the following year we find the burghers forming a new constitution, which came to be known as the *primo popolo*, led by a body of thirty-six headed by the *capitano del popolo*, independent of the nobles. Thus there were virtually two republics, the commune under the podestà and the *popolo* under its *capitano*. In 1260 the Florentine Guelfs were defeated by their Ghibelline opponents at the bloody battle of Montaperti and the city was only saved from destruction by the plea of the Ghibelline noble Farinata degli Uberti. In 1266 the Ghibellines in turn were expelled and the city was ruled by the Guelfs under the captain of the Guelf party. The richer elements (*popolo grasso*), grouped in the seven major guilds, under their own priors and councils, were steadily increasing their influence in state affairs; in 1289 the number of guilds was increased to twelve and then to twenty-one, seven *maggiori* and fourteen *minori*. In 1292 the famous Ordinances of Justice decreed that only those who were members of the *arti* could be members of the government. A gonfalonier of justice was appointed as a further check on the turbulence of the nobility. Factions among the upper classes led to the formation of two parties, known as the *Neri* (Blacks) and the *Bianchi* (Whites), and when the latter were defeated, one of those driven into exile was the poet Dante Alighieri (1302).

In 1325 a change was made in the constitution: a council of the people was formed, consisting of three hundred *popolani*, presided over by the *capitano del popolo*, and a council of the commune of 250 members, half from the nobility and half *popolani*, presided over by the podestà. This system was further democra-tized after 1343, when the nobles were excluded from the executive (the *gonfalo-niere* and the eight *priori*), but still allowed to serve as members of the council of the commune. Florence was now an oligarchic, commercial republic: the preponderance of the merchant class in control of affairs shaped its external policy, which was strongly Guelf, and not without good commercial reason, since its banking houses handled the finances of the papacy.

Prestanza cover, showing the *gonfalone* of the Quarter of Santo Spirito, Florence, 1408.

Rome. Part of a fresco
by Taddeo di Bartolo, 1414.

Rome   The position of Rome was anomalous in two important respects: firstly, the legal sovereignty over the city could be disputed between Popes, Emperors and citizens; secondly, it possessed little industry and consequently no powerful bourgeoisie. The population consisted of a fractious nobility and a numerous plebeian class, with only a thin layer of artisans and merchants in between. Yet in 1143 Rome also was infected with republican fervour; the people expelled the papal prefect and set up a senate under a 'patrician'. At this juncture there arrived in Rome an Augustinian monk, Arnold of Brescia, a pupil of Peter Abelard, who had been exiled from France and from his native city for preaching the return of the Church to its primal poverty and simplicity and the abolition of the temporal power of the papacy. Arnold provided the leadership the new commune required and for his heretical views was excommunicated by Pope Eugenius. Finally the English Pope Hadrian IV (1154–59), placing the city under interdict, secured the banishment of Arnold, who was taken prisoner by the Emperor Frederick I and handed over to the papal prefect for execution (1155). Although opposed by Popes and Emperors, the senate continued its existence in one form or another, so that papal or imperial pretensions to supremacy over the city had always to contend with the republicanism of the Romans.

The western seaport communes of Pisa and Genoa had gained great prosperity *Pisa and Genoa* under their consuls and councils, the aristocracy (particularly in Genoa) taking a leading part in commerce. In 1015 the allied fleets of Pisa and Genoa wrested Sardinia from the Moslems, but the subsequent capture of Corsica led to rivalry and war between the communes. The Balearic Isles fell to the Pisans in 1114; and in 1135 and 1137 their fleet destroyed Amalfi. The continued emnity with Genoa ultimately brought ruin to Pisa; on 6 August 1284 the fleets of the two cities met off Meloria, and the battle resulted in the almost complete annihilation of the Pisans. An alliance of the Florentines with the Lucchese and Genovese forced terms on Pisa which reduced her permanently to a subordinate political position; her splendid cathedral, baptistery, cemetery and the famous leaning tower remain as a memorial to her material greatness in the twelfth and thirteenth centuries.

Late thirteenth-century relief showing the port of Pisa. The harbour chains were captured by the Florentines in the fourteenth century and hung before their baptistery, until they were restored to Pisa in 1848.

Left: Palermo. The Norman royal court in the twelfth century. *Right:* Portrait of the Emperor Frederick Barbarossa (*c.* 1123–90).

In the kingdom of the Two Sicilies the formation of a unitary Norman state, while it did not prevent the enrichment of the seaport cities, meant the effective loss of their autonomy. Naples, which had reached such prosperity under its dukes, fell after a stubborn siege to Roger II in 1139; Palermo, however, remained the capital of the kingdom until after the Angevin conquest in 1265. The Normans inherited the magnificent civilization created by the Moslems of Sicily and further enriched it with enduring monuments of their own cosmopolitan taste. Under the Normans and their Hohenstaufen successors (1130–1266), the kingdom (*il regno*, as it became known) was by far the most economically advanced and (because of its highly centralized and efficient administration) richest state in the West.

The Kingdom of
the Two Sicilies

The essential unreality of the political claims of the kings of Germany to imperial sovereignty in Italy is illustrated by the career of the first Hohenstaufen Emperor, Frederick I, nicknamed Barbarossa (1155–90). In his person were reconciled

◀ Pisa. The façade of the Cathedral, 1063–92.

the houses of Welf and Waiblingen. He was no sooner secure of his position north of the Alps than he showed that he had taken to heart the teachings of the Bolognese school of Roman law, in which the successors of the great glossator Irnerius (d. 1125) were adapting to contemporary conditions the authoritarian imperial claims of the time of Justinian. According to these views the Emperor was universal and absolute sovereign, all powers stemmed from him, and the imperial rights were imprescriptible.

On the first of his six visits to Italy, in 1154, Barbarossa summoned the feudal magnates and representatives of the cities to an imperial diet at Roncaglia, near Piacenza. He denied the legality of the rights 'usurped' by the Lombard communes, and on their refusal to comply with his commands he ravaged the countryside around Milan, burnt Tortona, and handed over Asti and Chieri to the loyal marquis of Montferrat. At a second diet at Roncaglia he defined the imperial rights, or *regalia*: the authority to appoint civic authorities and judges, to coin money, to collect tolls, dues and supplies for his troops, and to dispose of duchies, marquisates and counties. He thereupon appointed his nominees as podestàs in the Lombard cities.

In 1161 Barbarossa with his German knights and Lombard allies took Milan after a long siege and razed it to the ground. Frederick's successes, however, were short-lived: in 1164 a league was formed against him in the Veronese (later known as the Trevisan) March by Verona, Vicenza, Padua and Treviso, with the support of Venice. This was the origin of the famous Lombard League, which was to ally most of the cities against the Emperor, to build Alessandria (insultingly named after his enemy the Pope), and finally to accomplish the decisive defeat of the imperialists at the battle of Legnano (29 May 1176), when the despised citizen militia ignominiously put to rout the Teutonic chivalry. At the Peace of Constance (1183) the Emperor had the political sagacity to acknowledge the inevitable: he recognized the League and granted the cities their constitutions, subject to a vague imperial suzerainty. The Italian cities in return were to provide the imperial army, when in Italy, with the *fodro* (supplies) and to accept the Emperor's representatives in matters of judicial appeal. In a Lateran Council of 1179 the conditions for papal elections were finally established – that candidate who received two-thirds of the votes of the consistory (the attendant cardinals) was elected Pope. The Emperor's confirmation was explicitly excluded.

By all this carnage and destruction Frederick had achieved nothing: where he failed by force of arms he was successful by diplomatic means. A dynastic

King William II, 'the Good', presents a model of the Cathedral of Monreale (1174) to the Virgin. Mosaic at Monreale.

alliance was made with the Norman ruler of the Two Sicilies. Frederick's eldest son, later the Emperor Henry VI (1191–97), married Constance, daughter of Roger II and heiress-presumptive to the childless William II (1166–89). On William's death, however, the Normans chose as king the illegitimate Tancred. When he died in 1193, Henry marched south and took captive the widowed Queen Sibilla and her young son, whom he sent to Germany and had blinded. The barons were brought to heel by acts of ruthless cruelty. In 1194 the Empress Constance gave birth at Jesi to a son, Frederick. The Popes were well aware of the danger that now threatened them from the north and south.

61

Pope Innocent III (Conti, *c.* 1160–1216, Pope, 1198).

Chapter Four

GUELFS, GHIBELLINES AND THE RISE OF THE DESPOTS, *c.* 1200–1350

The power of the medieval papacy reached its zenith in the pontificate of Innocent III (1198–1216), a scion of the Conti family, lords of Segni. A man of acute intelligence and of indefatigable energy, he found the text for his consecrational sermon in the words: 'See, I have today set thee over the nations and over the kingdoms, to pluck up and to break down, to destroy and to overthrow, to build and to plant.' And this proud claim he made good. He developed Gratian's *Decretum* (the *Concordia Discordantium Canonum, c.* 1150) by a series of his own decretals, which, taken with those of his successors, Honorius III, Gregory IX, Innocent IV and Boniface VIII, form the main body of canon law.

The year before Innocent's accession to the papal throne the Emperor Henry VI died. His son, Frederick, now aged two, had already been elected king of the Romans (that is, Emperor-presumptive) in 1196. In 1198 Frederick's mother died, leaving her son under the guardianship of Innocent III, whom she appointed regent of the Sicilies.

In Germany the electors, rejecting a regency for the young Frederick, revived the old Welf-Waiblingen conflict, and the country was rent by civil war, until the assassination of one of the contenders left Otto of Brunswick as the sole claimant. Innocent had not committed himself to either party and it was only at a stiff price that he crowned Otto as Emperor in Rome in 1209. The Romans, however, rose against the Germans. The Emperor Otto, seizing the pretext, refused to yield the Matildine territory, set up his own podestàs in northern Italy, invaded the Papal States and attempted the conquest of the Two Sicilies. Innocent replied by excommunicating him and by entering into negotiations with his adversaries in favour of his young ward Frederick of Hohenstaufen –

Incomincia il prohemio sopra li statuti delli uffitiali de...

I·nome sia della indiuidua trinita
padre figliuolo et spirito sancto et
della gloriosissima madre Madon
na Sancta Maria sempre uergine
madre del figliuolo di dio Padrona
et protectrice della Magnifica
Citta di Siena sotto ilnome della
quale ladetta citta di Siena si reg
ge et sigouerna. Et deprencipi degliapostoli Misser
Sancto Pietro et Misser Sancto Pauolo. Et degloriosi
martiri Misser Sancto Ansano. Sauino Crescentio et
Victorio et delglorioso confessore Sancto Bernardino

politically a policy fraught with danger to the papacy. The defeat of Otto, with his ally King John of England, by Philip Augustus of France at the battle of Bouvines (1214), led to his deposition by the German electors. Frederick, appearing north of the Alps, won over the support of the magnates and was crowned king of Germany at Aachen in 1215.

As a result of the Commercial Revolution, the papacy shared in the general increase of wealth. The Popes had early realized the convenience of the European ramifications of the nascent Italian capitalists, using first the Sienese, then the Florentine, banking houses to remit to Rome the papal funds. From England and Aragon and Sicily, as papal fiefs, came 'Peter's Pence'; from Sicily during the minority of Frederick were paid also the costs of 'administration'; from all over Europe were exacted the first fruits (*annates*) and tenths (tithes), the special taxation to finance the crusades, the fines and miscellaneous revenues. Finally, there was the income from the Papal States. This increase in material wealth provoked discontent, especially in the cities, at the privileges of the clergy, combined with vague utopian notions of bettering the conditions of the lower classes at the expense of the rich, both clerical and lay. And with this social discontent arose extreme heretical views.

Innocent acted vigorously against the diverse heretical sects of the time, for the Waldensians and the Cathars in particular seemed to threaten the very fabric of Christendom. Stern and unbending in his approach to the heretics, he nevertheless showed statesmanlike qualities in his recognition of the two Mendicant Orders – the Franciscans and the Dominicans – founded by Francis Bernardone (*c.* 1181–1226, canonized 1228) and Dominic Caleruega (1170–1221, canonized 1234). In these two contemporaneously founded Orders, the

Left: Miniature by Sano di Pietro. Officials of the Merchants Guild, from the Statuto della Mercanzia, Siena, 1472–75.

Right: Persecution of Waldensians. From *Histoire générale des églises évangeliques des vallées de Piemont ou vaudoises*, by J. Léger, 1669.

St Francis of Assisi (Francisco
Bernardone, c. 1181–1226). This
portrait is thought to have been
painted during his lifetime, c. 1220.

Commercial Revolution may be said to have created its religious outlet; and it
was natural that their houses were established mostly in the cities, where they
often became bitter rivals.

The harsh laws promulgated by Frederick II show that heresy was also rife in
the south. But in Provence and Languedoc still sterner measures were necessary
to stamp out Catharism: the Albigensian crusade (1209–15) laid waste the
lands of the troubadours amid scenes of unbelievable horror. Conformity was
achieved at the price of massacre and devastation, the crusaders creating a
wilderness in the name of orthodoxy. The Inquisition, in its harshest form, was
to follow. From the first the Dominicans were an intellectual foundation, whose
primary aim was to combat heresy. In 1244 Thomas Aquinas (1225–74,
canonized 1323), a son of the count of Aquino, entered the Order, after being a

St Dominic presiding over a court of
the Inquisition. From a painting by
Pedro Berruguete.

student at the newly formed University of Naples, from whence he moved to
Paris to study philosophy and theology under another Dominican, Albertus
Magnus. When, in 1233, Pope Gregory IX took the Inquisition (an ecclesiastical inquiry into charges of heresy) out of episcopal hands, thus forming what
became known as the Holy Office, it was to the Dominicans that he first entrusted the work of extirpating heresy.

Although Innocent had preached the fourth crusade (1202–04), his
attitude to the crusaders' capture of Zara and Constantinople, both events undertaken at the instigation of the Venetians, was ambiguous. First he excommunicated the Venetians; but when the crusaders acknowledged the Roman pontiff
as supreme over the Greek Church, he removed the ban, and his legate crowned
Baldwin of Flanders as first of the six Latin Emperors of the East (1204–61).

Frederick II   The achievements and the character of the Emperor Frederick II of Hohen-staufen (1194–1250) are difficult to assess; though in many ways he seems to have been so modern, yet in other respects he remains of his time, with his conception of imperial (if paternal) autocracy and his cruelty. Norman, Greek and Islamic elements were blended in Frederick's character – there seemed little of the German in him; and in fact he disliked his northern kingdom. Thirty-two years of his reign of forty years he passed in Italy. He was an enigma to his contemporaries: the Papal party, the Guelfs, saw him as Anti-Christ; others, like Matthew Paris, regarded him as *stupor mundi*, the 'wonder of the world'.

In the conflict of claims between the universality of Empire, put forward so forcibly by the Hohenstaufen Emperors from Frederick Barbarossa to his grand-son Frederick II, and the universality of things spiritual and their priority over matters temporal, especially as argued so vigorously by Popes from Innocent III to Boniface VIII, Italy played a central, dominant part: in the persons of the Emperor and his papal opponents the antagonists were both rulers of Italian states. If Frederick could call on the support of his German chivalry and his Moslem soldiery, the Popes, besides the weapons of excommunication and the proclaiming of a crusade, could find allies in the cities of the Lombard League.

Frederick had made a solemn vow to Innocent that he would not unite the crown of the regno with that of the Empire. Furthermore, he had taken the Cross in 1215. It was not until 1220 that he had arranged the affairs of Germany and received in Rome the imperial crown from Innocent's successor, Honorius (1216–27), renewing on this occasion his previous vow. For the next six years he was occupied in subduing the rebellious barons of Apulia and in putting down revolts of the Moslems in Sicily. Twenty thousand of the latter he settled at Lucera in Apulia, where they were allowed to practise their own religion, and to live under their own laws.

The Pope, alarmed at the measures Frederick was taking to strengthen his southern kingdom by the abolition of feudal abuses and the assertion of a central authority responsible directly to himself, extracted from him a further solemn pledge that he would set out on the long-delayed crusade by August 1227. The Emperor, however, was determined first to extend his dominion over the com-munes and feudality of central and northern Italy. For this purpose he summoned a diet at Cremona in March 1226. The formation of a second Lombard League, which blocked the passes through which his German reinforcements could enter Italy, thwarted his plans; and after placing the recalcitrant cities under the 'imperial ban' (which amounted virtually to nothing), he retired to Apulia.

The Emperor Frederick II
(Hohenstaufen, 1194–1250).

At this juncture the pacific Pope Honorius died and was succeeded by Gregory IX (1227–41), an old man of fierce temper and determined will. One of his first acts was to order the reluctant crusader to redeem his vow. The Emperor set sail on 8 September 1227, but an outbreak of malaria forced him to disembark at Otranto. Gregory immediately excommunicated him. Europe was kept informed of the charges and counter-charges in an angry battle of encyclicals and manifestoes. Nevertheless, Frederick set out in the following June, with the ban still upon him. Resorting to diplomacy, Frederick reached an agreement with the Egyptian Sultan Kemal, whereby Jerusalem, Bethlehem and Nazareth were once more opened to Christians. Then, crowning himself king of Jerusalem, which he claimed through his wife Yolande of Brienne, he returned to Apulia in 1229 and speedily drove the invading papal troops out of the Two Sicilies. Both sides now sought agreement and at length Pope and Emperor came to terms by the Treaty of San Germano, the ban being lifted from Frederick in return for some face-saving concessions to the Sicilian clergy.

The succeeding period, during which Frederick arranged the affairs of his southern kingdom, was the most constructive of his career. The late Professor Schipa has considered the Emperor Frederick II to have had no equal, among the rulers from Charlemagne to Napoleon. He founded the University of Naples in 1224. With the exception of a few members related to him by marriage

Gold *augustale* of Frederick II, obverse and (*below*) reverse.

From Frederick II's *De Artibus venandi cum avibus*, the first 'scientific' account of ornithology since antiquity.

(such as the counts of Aquino), he distrusted the southern nobility, and gathered around him as advisers and officials a brilliant group of men who owed their position solely to their ability and loyalty. Below them was a highly efficient bureaucracy, inspired by Arabic models, whose actions were reported to him twice a year at a meeting of the Three estates (barons, clergy and two representatives from forty-eight of the larger cities and towns of the kingdom). At such a meeting held at Melfi on 1 September 1231 he promulgated his famous *Liber* or *Lex Augustalis*. Justice was to be removed from the feudal courts and administered by the royal courts alone; it was also to be subject to strict review.

Like his Norman predecessors Frederick was a great builder. The shell which remains of his Castel del Monte in Apulia shows the refinement of his taste. (The flushing lavatories must have been some of the first to be constructed since antiquity.) In such delightful castles he held his cosmopolitan courts, surrounded by philosophers, mathematicians, 'scientists', musicians and poets, discussing all manner of subjects in any of the six languages in which he was fluent. His book on falconry, *De arte venandi cum avibus*, is the first modern natural history. At his court we witness the birth of Italian poetry, inspired first by Provençal models. Frederick himself, as well as his sons Enzio and Manfred, wrote verse in the vernacular; and so widespread was the fame of these courtly poets – Pier della Vigna (his secretary of state), Giacomo da Lentini (the 'Notary'), Rinaldo d'Aquino and Giacomo Pugliese – that all poetry written in Italian was for long known as 'Sicilian'.

Frederick was determined to assert the imperial authority over the peninsula and to curb the temporal power of the papacy, restricting the Popes to their spiritual functions. In this policy he overreached himself, for the Popes made common cause with the Lombard communes in resisting him. No Pope would accept the loss of the Papal States or the existence of a strong central power in Italy, since (it was argued) these circumstances would diminish his universal

◀ The Castel del Monte, Apulia, the most magnificent of Frederick II's many 'palaces of solace', *c*. 1240.

spiritual role and relegate the papacy to the status of the patriarchs of Constantinople. In northern and central Italy the towns or nobles who favoured Frederick or the Pope did so not from any strictly held doctrinal principle, but rather from the rivalries of communal particularism. Within the towns there arose factions which sought alliances to achieve power and to expel the opposing party. Hence every town had its groups of exiles (*fuorusciti*), awaiting the occasion to attack their native city in conjunction with the latter's Guelf or Ghibelline enemies. If successful, they expelled their opponents, until a reversal of fortune saw them once more in exile, and the whole process began again *da capo*.

Milan put herself at the head of a fresh anti-imperialist League in Lombardy: Pavia and Cremona, her natural rivals, served the Ghibelline interest. Of the nobility the marquis of Este was Guelf, because of his enmity with Ezzelino da Romano, who in 1232 had abandoned the League to become Frederick's lieutenant in the march of Verona. By 1236 Ezzelino had gained possession of Verona, Vicenza and Padua and had forced the marquis of Este and the powerful count of San Bonifazio to submit. The policy of the marquis of Montferrat was opportunist but in the main Guelfic, while the count of Savoy, poised on the passes between Savoy and Piedmont, held firm for the Emperor.

At the battle of Cortenuova, fought in November 1237, Milan, with her allies – Alessandria, Como, Crema, Vercelli, Piacenza and Novara – suffered an overwhelming defeat. It seemed that the Emperor's cause was triumphant: the captured Milanese *carroccio* was sent to adorn the Roman Capitol, a significant hint as to Frederick's ultimate intentions. Gregory IX, in these straits, made a secret treaty with the Venetians and Genoese, excommunicated the 'heretical' Emperor, and summoned a council in Rome. The Genoese convoy, with nearly a hundred prelates (including two cardinals) on board, was captured in 1241 near the Isle of Montecristo by Frederick's son Enzio and a fleet from Ghibelline Pisa. Later in the year the Emperor was on the outskirts and about to attack Rome when the aged Pope died.

After Celestine IV's short reign of seventeen days, there was an interregnum before the cardinals elected Sinibaldo de' Fieschi, a Genoese noble, who took the name of Innocent IV (1243–54). With the assistance of his compatriots Innocent fled from Rome, arriving by sea at Genoa on 7 July 1244, and from there travelling to Lyons, where he convoked a general council, which excommunicated and deposed the Emperor, absolving his subjects from their oaths of allegiance. The Mendicant Orders were violent in their attacks upon Frederick's morals; his harem, his eunuchs and semi-oriental court, his Moslem soldiery, his menagerie – even the fact of his taking a daily bath – were invoked against him. It was given out that he was an unbeliever, and plots were hatched to assassinate him and his sons. The Moslems of Sicily were instigated to revolt. Relatives of the Pope persuaded the hitherto imperialist Parma to rise against Frederick, and in the siege that followed, the Emperor, caught off his guard, suffered a serious setback, when a sudden sally of the besieged destroyed his camp and captured his treasury. In November 1250 the Emperor Frederick, worn out at the age of fifty-six, died at his hunting-lodge of Fiorentino in Apulia. 'Let the heavens rejoice and the earth exult,' wrote the Vicar of Christ on receiving the report.

In papal eyes the paramount necessity was to extirpate 'the viper's brood', the surviving Hohenstaufen. When Frederick's heir Conrad died in 1254, the regency for Conrad's child Conradin was undertaken by Frederick's youngest (illegitimate) son Manfred, who was shortly after proclaimed king of the Two Sicilies and leader of the Ghibelline party, which was now again in the ascend-ant throughout central and northern Italy. On the defeat and death of the notorious Ezzelino da Romano in 1259, the leadership of the imperialists in Lombardy fell to Uberto Pelavicini; and even the Guelf faction in Milan, led by the family of della Torre, felt obliged to appoint him captain-general of the city for five years. In Romagna and Tuscany Manfred's cause was ably conducted by his 'vicars'. At the battle of Montaperti (September 1260) his general, Count Jordan of Anglano, at the head of the Ghibellines of Siena, supported by the Florentine exiles under Farinata degli Uberti, gained a decisive victory against the Guelfs of Florence, which resulted in the city's submission to a Ghibelline podestà, Count Guido Novello, who ruled as Manfred's vicar until 1266.

As a desperate remedy to this deterioration in Guelfic affairs a French Pope, Urban IV (1261–64), closed the prolonged negotiations with the ambitious Charles of Anjou and Provence, inviting him to invade the kingdom of the Sicilies. This expedition, promoted to the status of a crusade by Urban's successor, Clement IV (1264–68), set out in 1265. As senator of Rome and champion of the Italian Guelfs, Charles was crowned king of the Two Sicilies in St Peter's in February 1266. In the same month Manfred was defeated and killed outside Benevento. The end of the house of Hohenstaufen came two years later, when the young Conradin crossed the Alps to regain his kingdom. Overcome by Charles of Anjou at Tagliacozzo and taken prisoner as he tried to escape, he expiated his crime of *lèse-majesté* on a scaffold in the Piazza del Mercato in Naples (29 October 1268).

Charles of Anjou, King Charles I of
Naples, 1266–82.

Within four years Charles's power, as leader of the Guelfs, was paramount
in Italy. One of the results of this change was that papal policy under Gregory
X (1271–76) and Nicholas III (1277–80) became distinctly Ghibelline – a fair
illustration of the looseness of these terms. Firmly in possession of the regno,
Charles was elected (1268) senator of Rome for ten years. Florence expelled
Count Guido; with the Guelfs once more in the saddle the *signoria* (lordship)
of the city was offered to Charles, whom Pope Clement had appointed vicar-
imperial in Tuscany. In Milan he had already been given the *signoria* by the
leading family of della Torre, and he also held this position in a number of
towns in Piedmont. In Lombardy he was *signore* (with the power to appoint the
podestàs and control foreign policy) in Parma, Piacenza, Reggio, Modena,
Cremona, Alessandria and Brescia.

Charles's ambitious plans to conquer Constantinople received a fatal setback, however, when in the episode of the Sicilian Vespers (31 March 1282)
the people of Palermo rose against the French and expelled from the island those
who escaped the massacres. Sicily then passed into the power of King Pedro of
Aragon, the husband of Manfred's daughter. All Charles's efforts to reconquer
it were in vain; and ultimately the separation of Sicily (thenceforth officially
known as the kingdom of Trinacria) from Naples was recognized by the Treaty
of Caltabellotta (1302).

The Sicilian Vespers, 13 March 1282. Soldiers of the period, from a thirteenth-century
French MS.

French Supremacy,
and the Rise
of the Despots

The period which followed was characterized by two marked tendencies: the increasing predominance of France in Italian affairs, and the replacement of republican institutions in the cities of northern and central Italy by the rule of a single individual or a family. We have arrived at the 'Age of the Despots', an age which saw the rise of the *condottieri*, the mercenary leaders of armed bands (*compagnie di ventura*, 'companies of adventure'), who themselves frequently founded dynasties. Of the early *compagnie di ventura* the most famous (and feared) were the Company of St George under Lodrisio Visconti, the Great Company of the German Duke Werner, the company commanded by the ex-Templar known as Fra Moriale, and the White Company captained by the Englishman John Hawkwood.

The last of the great medieval pontiffs, the imperious Cardinal Gaetani, who took the name of Boniface VIII (1294–1303), had a conception of the papacy no less exalted than that of Innocent III, but lacked entirely the latter's judgment. What was in the nature of a personal vendetta against the Roman family of Colonna he proclaimed as a crusade. If his invitation to Charles of Valois to intervene in Sicily and in Florence was a failure, his quarrel with

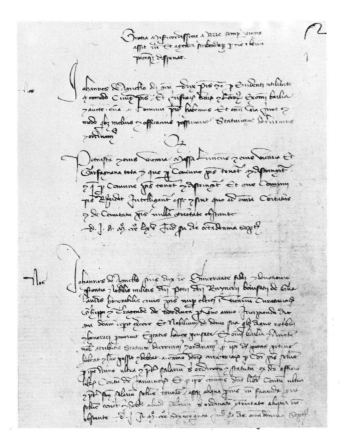

Note of payment by the city of Lucca to the condottiere Sir John Hawkwood and his company of mercenaries, 7 October 1375.

Pope Boniface VIII (Gaetani)
with two cardinals.
Attributed to Giotto.

Philip the Fair of France was nothing less than a disaster. Immersed in the petty politics of Italian states, he was in no position to understand the consolidation of the new secular monarchy beyond the Alps. In his bull *Clericis laicos* (1296) he declared the French clergy immune from royal taxation. When Philip immediately put an embargo on the export of gold to Italy, Boniface was compelled to listen to the complaints of the hard-hit Florentine bankers and to retract. Yet he refused to modify his extremist claims: 'Indeed we declare, announce and define that it is altogether necessary to salvation for every human creature to be subject to the Roman pontiff.' This is the gist of his famous bull *Unam sanctam* (1302).

Philip convoked a council in Lyons (1303), and despatched Guillaume de Nogaret and two exiled Colonna brothers to fetch the Pope, if necessary by force. They found Boniface in his palace at Anagni, and Nogaret had to restrain Sciarra Colonna from murdering him. The Pope, rescued by the populace two days later, was escorted by a troop of Orsini horse to Rome; but it is said that the humiliation was too much for his proud spirit, for within a month he was dead. Two years later the choice of the cardinals fell on a Frenchman, Bertrand de Goth (Clement V, 1305–13), who immediately created nine

Palace of the Popes at Avignon. Seventeenth-century wash drawing.

French cardinals. In 1309 he moved the papal court to Avignon and the long 'Babylonian Captivity' (1309–77) began, a period when all the Popes, and most of the cardinals, were French, and the French king's influence was supreme. In Dante's scathing phrase, the Popes 'went whoring with the kings'.

From the final eclipse of the Hohenstaufens in 1268 and the revival of the Guelfs with the advent of Charles of Anjou, no Emperor crossed the Alps to assert the imperial claims in Italy until the coming of Henry VII in 1310, an event hailed with almost mystical fervour by Dante among the more moderate Ghibel-lines. The failure of Henry's intervention in Italian affairs – he aimed at the reconciliation of Guelf with Ghibelline and the restoration of the exiles to their native cities – revealed the emergence of a new balance of forces during the preceding half-century. Earlier, as we have seen, the middle classes in the communes had curbed the nobles of the *contado*, enforcing a period of residence within the cities and in various ways (such as the Florentine Ordinances of Justice of 1292) limiting their political power. Yet the power of the nobility was now strengthened by the development of military tactics. The almost continual inter-communal warfare constituted a heavy burden on the citizen levies, who had to support themselves during the campaigns, and who suffered

Captains of *compagnie di ventura* receiving the pay.

the loss from the interruption to their employment. Further, the nobility and the richer burghers alone possessed the wealth and the leisure which the training of mail-clad cavalry demanded. In the open field the citizen militia was no longer a match for the horse-borne nobles and their well-armed and trained retainers. Such circumstances brought about the appearance of the professional soldier, both noble and plebeian.

These conditions – inter-communal warfare, the internal life of the city a prey to the tumults of faction, the preponderance of the nobility over the burghers in the profession of arms – all favoured the rise of the despots in the cities of northern and (later) central Italy. However the despot achieved his *signoria*, whether by a coup, by heading a successful faction, by invitation, by conquest, or even by purchase, the general characteristics of his rule were similar. Although he might retain the semblance of the old republican institutions, the effective power in the state was in his hands alone, backed by mercenaries. Any suspicion of disaffection was met with exile, imprisonment or execution. The middle classes, if deprived of a voice in government, profited by the greater security and social tranquillity; in the lower classes (*popolo minuto*) the despot as a rule found his most solid support. The very insecurity of his status (even if for a cash pay-ment he obtained *de jure* recognition from Emperor or Pope) led him to cast

The Visconti family tree. First half of the fifteenth century.

his eyes on neighbouring cities and to seek to extend his dominion, thereby transforming the city-state into the regional state.

With the exception of the della Scala dynasty (the Scaligers), who became *signori* of Verona after the defeat of Ezzelino da Romano in 1259, the earliest despots were almost invariably nobles. In 1278 the 'Great Marquis' William of Montferrat was *signore* or war-captain (or some such equivalent title) of Casale, Tortona, Alessandria, Turin, Ivrea, Crema, Pavia, Milan, Vercelli and Novara. The long-protracted struggle in Milan between the two noble families of della Torre (Guelf) and Visconti (Ghibelline) for the *signoria* of the city ended in victory for the latter; in the persons of Archbishop Otto Visconti and his nephew Matteo (created vicar-imperial by Henry VII in 1311) began that remarkable dynasty which brought Milan into the forefront of Italian, and indeed European, politics.

In Lombardy there followed a period of consolidation, which witnessed the process of transformation of communal into regional states, many of the Padane cities passing into the control of three prominent dynasties. Foremost were the Visconti, who became lords of Milan, Pavia, Como, Bergamo, Lodi, Cremona, among other cities and territories. The Scaligers, of whom the greatest was Can Grande della Scala (d. 1329), the friend of Dante, held the *signoria* of Verona, Vicenza, Parma, Feltre, Belluno and Treviso. The ancient feudal house of Este, Germanic in origin, were masters of the cities of Ferrara, Modena and Comacchio. Mantua, the scene of violent conflicts between the counts of San Bonifazio and the Bonaccorsi, finally came into the possession of Luigi Gonzaga in 1328. In Padua the *signoria* was held by the Carraresi.

The Guelf cities of Piedmont owed their comparative immunity from the general strife to the protection of the Neapolitan Angevins, until the death of King Robert in 1393, when they were partitioned between the count of Savoy, the marquis of Montferrat and the Visconti of Milan. Bologna struggled to maintain its precarious republican freedom against the Visconti, the temporary despotism of Taddeo de' Pepoli, and the papacy, only falling to the Bentivoglio at the beginning of the fifteenth century.

The Ghibelline Castruccio Castracane, lord of Lucca, Pisa and Pistoia, was on the point of making himself master of Tuscany, when death cut short his career (1328). Three years previously he had defeated the Florentines with such heavy loss at the battle of Altopascio that they were obliged to offer the *signoria* to Charles of Calabria, son of King Robert. The petty states of Romagna and the Marches were almost entirely in the hands of despots: the Malatesta at

Proclamation of Marsilio da Carrara as Signore of Padua, and the presentation of the city's standard, 1337.

Cardinal Albornoz receiving homage from the reconquered Papal States. Mid-fourteenth century.

Rimini, the da Polenta at Ravenna, the Ordelaffi at Forlì, the Manfredi at Faenza, the Varano at Camerino, and the distinguished family of Montefeltro at Urbino. Farther south, in Umbria, the largest commune, Perugia, though seldom free from factional troubles instigated chiefly by the Baglioni, was seeking to extend its dominion over Foligno, Spoleto and Assisi and was contending with Arezzo and Siena for possession of Cortona and Montepulciano.

Rome Rome, deprived of its main source of income by the absence of the Popes, had fallen into anarchy, a prey to the dissensions arising from class-divisions and the incessant quarrels of the nobility grouped around the Guelfic Orsini and Ghibel-line Colonna. Once again the cure was sought in the resuscitation of ancient forms, with the appointment of an idealistic demagogue, Cola di Rienzo, a *popolano*, as 'tribune of the Roman republic'. Filled with notions partly of classical Rome, partly of a messianic nature, he roused the people to expel the nobles, who were defeated in an engagement beneath the city walls (1347). His call to the cities of Italy to unite met with a measure of approval (Petrarch was at first enthusiastic); but megalomania and certain weaknesses of character, revealed in moments of crisis, antagonized his supporters and led to his downfall and death at the hands of the Roman mob (1354). Cardinal Albornoz was sent by Pope Innocent VI (1352–62) into the Papal States to restore papal rule, which almost everywhere had been usurped by despots from the local nobility. In this task he showed remarkable talents, establishing papal governors in the cities; in Rome he appointed a foreign senator to administer the city in the Pope's name.

King Robert (1309–43) was succeeded in the kingdom of Naples by his young granddaughter Joanna I (1343–81), but her accession to the throne was marked by the outbreak of a fratricidal conflict between the Durazzo and the Taranto branches of the house of Anjou. Joanna had married her cousin Andrew, the brother of King Louis I of the Angevin house of Hungary. On the murder of Andrew at Aversa (1345) and Joanna's remarriage with Louis of Taranto, the king of Hungary invaded the Neapolitan kingdom. Joanna and Louis fled to Avignon, where she managed to clear herself before the Pope of complicity in Andrew's murder, at the price of ceding her rights to Avignon. The war dragged on, causing devastation to the kingdom; and although Joanna succeeded in retaining her throne, the end of hostilities found the territorial nobility virtually independent of royal authority.

The Kingdom of Naples

In the mid-fourteenth century there began those terrible periodic visitations of plague from the East. Gabriel de Mussis, an Italian lawyer, described how he travelled from the Crimea in a ship which docked in Genoa late in 1347, bringing with it the Black Death. Many of the crew died *en route* from what appears to have been a bubonic variety of the disease, and so powerful was the virus that the survivors infected the inhabitants of Genoa. With terrifying rapidity the Black Death spread over northern and central Italy. According to contemporary calculations one-third of the population of Italy perished, Boccaccio giving the dead in Florence alone at a hundred thousand, which is certainly an exaggeration. Recurrences of the plague (not necessarily bubonic), particularly those of 1363 and 1374, brought further widespread depopulation, especially in the crowded cities, and the consequence was a serious disruption of social bonds.

The Plague

The Black Death. Flagellants doing penance to avoid contagion.

Chapter Five

RENAISSANCE, *c.* 1250–1494

As we have seen, the thirteenth-century court of the Emperor Frederick II in Sicily and southern Italy already presents evidence of cultural pursuits which two centuries later would be regarded as the hallmark of the Renaissance. In architecture and sculpture Frederick initiated movements of cardinal import-ance; and here he looked back in order to move forward. The Commercial Revolution in the communes, and the consolidation of a Norman kingdom in the south, had brought great advances in material prosperity, which resulted in communal endeavours hitherto unattempted: firstly, the building, by public subscription, of splendid Romanesque churches, followed in the next century by the Gothic *palazzo pubblico*, that fullest outward expression of municipal life.

The plan adopted for these churches was with few exceptions the Roman basilica. In the north the style was predominantly Lombard-Romanesque: S. Ambrogio, Milan (*c.* 850, but partly rebuilt, with atrium, 1128); S. Michele, Pavia (1117); S. Zeno Maggiore, Verona (1139); and among secular buildings the Fondaco dei Turchi (twelfth century, but rebuilt); the Palazzi Loredan and Farsetti (both twelfth century) in Venice; and such fortified towers as the Torre Asinelli in Bologna (1109). In central Italy the Cathedral of Pisa (1063–92), on the plans of the Greek Boschetto, with its veneers of red and white marble, was the progenitor of the Pisan-Romanesque style. Other churches of the period include S. Miniato, Florence (1013, but rebuilt 1140); the Badia, Fiesole (façade *c.* 1090); the Cathedral, S. Michele and S. Frediano, Lucca (all twelfth century); and the Cathedral, Pistoia (*c.* 1170).

In southern Italy, as was to be expected from its position at the meeting-place of Byzantine and Arab cultures, the Norman builders of the great

◀ The façade of S. Michele, Lucca (from 1143). This upper gable is a mere screen.

Head from the pulpit in Ravello Cathedral.
Attributed to Niccolò di Bartolommeo da
Foggia (c. 1200?).

cathedrals, especially of Sicily and Apulia, incorporated elements of Eastern architecture and decoration (Saracenic arches, interlaced arcading and Byzantine mosaics) in structures which were essentially Romanesque. Of great interest and beauty are the Cappella Palatina (1132) in Palermo, and the cathedrals of Monreale and Cefalù. The prototype of Apulian-Romanesque was S. Nicola, Bari (1105), which was closer than Sicilian building to the Lombard style; others, among the many fine churches of Apulia, are the cathedrals of Bari (after 1170), Trani (1159 and later) and Bitonto (1175). The façade of Troia Cathedral, also in Apulia, suggests the presence of a Pisan architect. In these southern Romanesque churches we find many beautiful examples of baldacchini, ambones and paschal candlesticks in marble inlaid with brilliant glass mosaic, similar to the contemporary work of the Roman family of Cosmati.

Frederick's interest lay not in ecclesiastical architecture, but in the building of fortresses, palaces and hunting-lodges – his 'palaces of solace'. For this purpose he employed French and Lombard masons, whom he brought together in the workshops of Foggia and Capua. The sculpture which was there produced shows the influence of French Gothic, but, even more significant for the future, it reveals a conscious revival of classical forms. The Capuan Gate, built by Frederick, was adorned with busts, which were in imitation of the colossal figures of late antiquity. The striking female head (1272) on the pulpit in the Cathedral of Ravello is the work of a known member of Frederick's ateliers, Niccolò di Bartolommeo da Foggia. There is every likelihood that in this circle around Niccolò was trained the artist who rediscovered and transmitted to his successors the sculptural plasticity of the ancients – Nicola Pisano (c. 1210– c. 1278).

87

◄ Monreale Cathedral. Columns of the cloisters; twelfth century.
Note the inlays of mosaic, the intricate capitals and the delicate tracery.

Nothing provides clearer evidence of the intellectual needs arising out of the Commercial Revolution than the widespread foundation of universities in the Italian cities at about the turn of the twelfth century. Besides Salerno (which has claims to be the oldest European university) and Naples in the south, by 1250 we find numerous universities in the cities of northern and central Italy: in Bologna, Reggio (Emilia), Modena, Vicenza, Padua, Vercelli, Piacenza, Pavia (perhaps), Parma and Arezzo. Somewhat later were the foundations of Perugia, Rome, Treviso (its duration was short), Pisa, Florence (until 1472, when it moved to Pisa), Siena and Ferrara.

Although Latin was the language of the Church, the schools, the courts, diplomacy and the learned, the thirteenth century saw the birth of a literature in the vernacular, which at first found a rival in French (Marco Polo's *Milione*, *c.* 1299, was written in French, as was the much-read *Trésor* by Dante's master, Brunetto Latini). But the native language (*volgare*) rapidly gained ground, and in the Tuscan verse and prose of the three great Florentines – Dante Alighieri (1265–1321), Petrarch (1304–74) and Boccaccio (1313–75) – achieved a splendid maturity. By writing in the Tuscan *volgare* as an act of deliberate decision, Dante set the seal on Tuscan as the language of cultivated Italians, while Petrarch's searches for lost works of the great Roman writers led to

Lecture in law given by Pietro da Unzola (d. *c.* 1312) at the University of Bologna.

Left: The beginning of Dante's *Inferno*, with a portrait of Dante and showing Virgil with Dante in the initial letter. *Right:* Petrarch. Detail from Raphael's 'Parnassus' in the Stanze in the Vatican (1509–12?).

valuable discoveries and were continued by his humanist successors. Boccaccio's supreme contribution to Italian letters lay in the development of a carefully cultivated, yet seemingly effortless, prose style, at once sinewy, limpid and singularly expressive.

The Sicilian school of poetry found a well-prepared audience in the Tuscan cities and in Bologna; already there existed in the language of the *Cantico delle creature* of St Francis a vehicle admirably adapted to poetic use – simple, yet full of feeling and movement. In the tortured, ecstatic outbursts of his Franciscan follower Jacopone da Todi (1236–1306) there sound the echoes of the Flagellant movement, of the *laudi sacre*, which were to develop in Umbria into the popular religious drama. But it required something radically different to bring about the full flowering of the Italian poetical imagination. Within a remarkably short space of time was produced a wholly new style of lyrical poetry, the *dolce stil nuovo*. The poetry of Guittone d'Arezzo (d. 1294), the young woman who goes by the name of the Compiuta Donzella (d. *c.* 1328), Guido Guinizelli of Bologna (d. 1276), Guido Cavalcanti (d. 1300), Lapo Gianni (d. *c.* 1328) and Cino da Pistoia (d. 1337) – this lyrical outburst culminated in the *Vita Nuova* and *Canzoniere* of Dante.

Scenes from Boccaccio's *Decameron*. From a *cassone* (marriage chest), attributed to Rossello di Jacopo Franchi.

If Dante reveals himself always as the aristocrat – proud, contemptuous, passionately involved – both Petrarch and Boccaccio no less clearly voice the interests, feelings and emotions of the ascending middle class. It was in the sequences of Italian sonnets and *canzoni* that Petrarch portrayed the new age: one in which men were entering into the full enjoyment of the natural world as revealed through the senses; but none the less one in which, from the very intensity of their introspection, the more sensitive spirits found themselves vulnerable to doubts, velleities, a debilitating malaise. In Boccaccio we find nothing of this, but rather the down-to-earth qualities of the Florentine burgher, hard-headed (or, at least, nimble-witted), libertine, somewhat coarse-grained, redeemed from worldliness by a certain religiosity and a lively appreciation of beauty. But Dante lives for all the peoples who share European culture as the first great poet since antiquity and among the greatest of all time in his *Divine Comedy*, written during the exile from which he never returned.

The Fine Arts The growth of material wealth from the eleventh century onwards brought with it a reviving interest in the fine arts, and, as we have already remarked, the first of these in time and importance was architecture. In Romanesque churches sculpture was essentially decorative and subordinate to architectural elements and composition. The decoration of buildings devoted to religious uses required, both externally and internally, sculpture, mosaics and frescoes that served a didactic rather than a purely aesthetic purpose. The hieratic stylization of the Byzantine tradition in painting and mosaics, and the technique of under-cutting with a drill in the carving which prevailed widely in Italy, gave way to a

90

Giovanni Pisano, 'The Elect at the Judgment', from the pulpit in ▶
Pisa Cathedral, 1302–10.

more plastic treatment of natural forms. Here the native tendencies of the work-shops of Lombard and Gothic sculptors were strengthened by the rediscovery of classical sculpture. From the second half of the twelfth century French sculptors were directed to the natural beauty of classical art by the study of Roman models (in Provence) and by a direct observation of nature (in northern France).

Sculpture increasingly broke away from its architectural setting, eventually to stand forth in its own right. In the latter half of the thirteenth century the Italian Gothic sculptors, notably the Pisani and their Tuscan followers, were so imbued with the spirit derived from the study of antique models as to form a new figurative language, capable of transcending imitation and of creating a wholly personal style.

And where sculptors led painters were soon to follow. For Byzantine linearity and iconography was substituted the representation of three-dimensional figures in space; and the scenes depicted, although almost entirely sacred in subject, were now of the everyday world. In the arts the influence of different techniques was reciprocal, a natural consequence when artists were more often than not practitioners in several branches, whether in sculpture, architecture, painting or the crafts of the goldsmith or worker in bronze.

Gothic ecclesiastical architecture was introduced into Italy from Burgundy by the Cistercians, who built the abbey church at Fossanova in 1187, followed by that of S. Galgano near Florence, the latter serving as the pattern for the

Cathedral of Siena (1226–1377). In Florence and Venice both Dominicans and Franciscans erected Gothic churches; and in the former city the architect-sculptor Arnolfo di Cambio, Nicola Pisano's pupil, began the rebuilding of the Cathedral of S. Maria del Fiore in 1296; Giotto's campanile was raised some forty years later. There is but a single example of the Gothic in Rome, S. Maria sopra Minerva (1285). However, the Angevin conquest of the Two Sicilies brought French Gothic architects to Naples; Charles and Robert of Anjou built castles as well as churches, employing in their decoration not only French artists but also Tuscan – Tino di Camaino, Giotto, Simone Martini, and the Roman Pietro Cavallini. In Venice Gothic secular architecture developed its own style, with its delicate open-work tracery, which is seen in the Doge's Palace (from 1309) and the famous Ca' d'Oro. The greatest monument to the Gothic style in Italy is Milan Cathedral, begun in 1386; but this building clearly illustrates that the verticality of Gothic was alien to Latin taste. However, it was in sculpture and painting that the influence of the northern Gothic artists had its greatest effect, and the ultimate victory of the native styles was achieved only as the outcome of a long but fruitful tension.

The Lombard sculptors of the twelfth century – Guglielmo in Modena and Benedetto Antelami in Parma – reveal an acquaintance with the antique; but it was a century later, in Pisa, that the fusion of Gothic and classical elements in Nicola Pisano's pulpit for the baptistery (*c.* 1260) pointed to the direction in which Italian sculptors would thenceforth advance. Associated with Nicola and his son Giovanni (d. *c.* 1320) were Arnolfo di Cambio (d. *c.* 1302),

Left: Giotto's rejected design for the campanile of the Cathedral at Florence (S. Maria del Fiore).

Right: Jacopo della Quercia, 'The Expulsion from Paradise', S. Petronio, Bologna.

92

The Ca' d'Oro, Venice. Architect, Bartolomeo Buon (d. 1464).

Tino di Camaino (d. 1337), Lorenzo Maitani (d. 1330), Andrea Pisano (d. 1348) and his son Nino (d. *c.* 1368). Also of the Tuscan school were Orcagna (active 1344–68), Ghiberti (1378–1455), Nanni di Banco (d. 1481) and Jacopo della Quercia of Siena (d. 1438).

When in 1401 the Arte di Calamala held a competition to award the commission for the design of a second pair of doors for the baptistery in Florence (the first pair was by Andrea Pisano), the award went to Ghiberti. One of the artists who had competed was Filippo Brunelleschi (1377–1446). Disappointed in his failure to gain the commission, Brunelleschi set out for Rome, accompanied by the young Donatello, to study antique remains at the fountain-head. The work of Donatello (1386–1466) and Brunelleschi (who later turned to architecture)

93

Mary Magdalen,
by Donatello.

marks the full classical revival; but how strong the pull of the Gothic sculptural style still was may be seen even at a late stage in Donatello's life, in, for example, his St Mary Magdalen in the Florentine baptistery. The influence of Ghiberti, and more particularly of Donatello, established the primacy of Florentine sculpture, as seen in the work of such artists as the Rossellino brothers, Desiderio da Settignano, Mino da Fiesole, Benedetto da Maiano, Luca della Robbia, Verrocchio and Pollaiuolo. From Florence the influence spread throughout Italy: in Naples and Urbino, among the more prominent sculptors were Luciano and Francesco Laurana; in Venice (where Gothic styles lingered), Bartolomeo Buon, Antonio Rizzo, the architect-sculptors Pietro and Tullio Lombardo and the Florentine-born Sansovino.

In painting also we find a similar opposition between the flowing linearity and the aesthetic exquisiteness of the courtly style, which is now known as International Gothic, and the reassertion of the primacy of the rendering of the human figure in space, which was the great achievement of Renaissance artists both in Flanders and in Italy. Modern European painting is said to have begun with Giotto (1266–1337), in that he, following the Tuscan sculpture, sought a new plasticity of natural forms. But Giotto only carried further what was already being attempted by others: his own master Cimabue (c. 1240–c. 1302), especially after his visits to Rome and Assisi; Pietro Cavallini, who turned to the early Christian (and thereby to classical) art which he saw round him in Rome; and the painters of Siena, the followers of Duccio di Buoninsegna, Simone Martini and the brothers Lorenzetti.

It has been said that the work of these masters at the beginning of the four-teenth century determined the character of Italian art for a hundred years to come. The Gothic church of S. Francesco at Assisi and the Arena Chapel at Padua are virtually galleries for the narrative series in fresco by Giotto and his assistants, which spread the knowledge of his style so widely that there grew up an academic school of 'Giotteschi'. The Sienese painters were more open to French influence; Simone Martini worked at the Angevin court of Naples and at the papal court in Avignon, at that time an important centre of the International Gothic style. Ambrogio Lorenzetti combined Giotto's naturalism with the refinement of colour and draughtsmanship of his master Duccio. Furthermore, at the court of the Visconti in Milan, at the University of Bologna, and in Verona the Franco-Flemish miniature painters were much admired for the elegant curvi-linear style, the sumptuous Burgundian dress, the courtly polish and the minia-turists' realism of detail in their works. The result was a diffusion of International

The International Gothic Style in Italy. 'St George and the Princess', by Pisanello, *c.* 1437.

Gothic through such painters as Gentile da Fabriano (d. 1427), Altichiero and Stefano da Zevio, Michelino da Besozza, Giovanni da Milano, Lorenzo Monaco and Pisanello (d. 1455). The Gothic style long constituted an element in Italian painting and sculpture: the sinuous movement of elongated forms and flowing drapery, the stylized elegance, the purely decorative use of highly rendered flowers and foliage find an echo in Fra Angelico, Domenico Veneziano, Agostino di Duccio, Botticelli, and even in the perspective-haunted Uccello.

Another of these Gothicizing painters, Masolino (d. 1447), was associated with the young Masaccio (b. 1401), the friend of Brunelleschi and Donatello, who, dying at the age of twenty-seven and leaving few pictures, turned Florentine painting into the track the sculptors had prepared for it – in the realization of harmonious human figures, rhythmically grouped according to aerial perspective by the graduated interplay of light. The Brancacci Chapel in the Carmine Church became the school for Italian painters. This fruitful intermingling of the

95

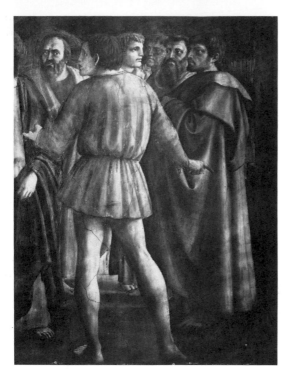

Left: Masaccio, 'The Tribute Money' (detail), from the Brancacci Chapel, Sta Maria del Carmine, Florence.

Right: Madonna and Child, by Verrocchio (1435–88).

Far right: Mary Magdalen, by Perugino.

influences of Donatello and Masaccio produced a succession of painters and sculptors hardly, if ever, equalled: Fra Filippo Lippi, Botticelli, Andrea del Sarto, Ghirlandaio, Michelangelo Buonarotti (Ghirlandaio's great pupil, 1475–1564), Pollaiuolo, the sculptor-painter Verrocchio, and Leonardo da Vinci (1452–1519), who was apprenticed in Verrocchio's studio. The Florentines influenced the painters of the Umbrian schools, by whom was perfected the rendering of the effects of light in spatial composition: Piero della Francesca and his pupil Signorelli. Another stream of Tuscan influence ran from Fra Angelico (d. 1455), through Benozzo Gozzoli, to Pinturicchio (d. 1513) and to the school of Perugia, where Perugino (d. 1524) was the master of Raphael Sanzio of Urbino (1483–1520).

From Florence also came fresh stimuli to the schools of Milan, Bologna, Ferrara and Parma – the last being famous for Correggio (d. 1534). Padua produced Mantegna (1431–1506), the brother-in-law to the true founder of the Venetian school, Giovanni Bellini (1430–1516). The Vivarini from Murano and the Bellini were two important families of painters, Giovanni Bellini's father, Jacopo (d. 1470), and his younger brother, Gentile (d. 1507), being notable figures. Associated with Gentile Bellini was Carpaccio (d. 1522). It was in the studio of Giovanni Bellini that Antonello da Messina (d. 1493)

introduced the Flemish invention of painting in oils, which made possible the magnificent exuberance of colour and light for which the Venetians were to be unsurpassed. Pupils of Giovanni were Titian (1477–1576) and the mysterious, romantic Giorgione, who died at the age of thirty-two in 1510.

At the time of the Renaissance art was not separate from, or opposed to, science; both pursuits were of one and the same thing. Nor were there 'two cultures'. Art was primarily the representation, or reconstruction, of visual reality; but in this the Florentines were much more intellectual than the Flemings. The Italians constructed their visual world according to intellectual principles, such as perspective and anatomy, which had to be discovered and mastered. Proportion and harmony were matters of mathematics. In this the architects were the first theorists, with their rationalization of forms, which they reduced to number and proportion. Ghiberti was only expressing accepted opinion when he wrote that a painter required to know grammar, arithmetic, geometry, philosophy, medicine, astrology, perspective, history, anatomy, 'theory' and drawing. In subscribing and adding to these desiderata Leonardo da Vinci moved on from being primarily an artist to the painstaking observation of nature and to the tentative formulation of scientific experiments and generalizations. What he found in

97

nature was structure and process, both susceptible of measurement. 'There is no certainty where one can neither apply any of the mathematical sciences nor any of those which are based on the mathematical sciences.' Piero della Francesca gave up painting for the last fourteen years of his life, so absorbed had he become in mathematics. Luca da Pacioli, Leonardo's friend, wrote in *De divina proportione* that he had found the secret of proportion in the Golden Section.

A part, but only a part, of this intellectualizing must be attributed to the humanists. By the mid-fifteenth century Vitruvius' lost book on architecture, *De re aedificatoria,* had been discovered; but it was chiefly in the work of practising artists that the problems were posed and solutions were found: L. B. Alberti (1404–72) wrote on sculpture, painting and architecture; Ghiberti published his *Commentaries,* and Piero della Francesca his *De prospetiva pingendi.* Men were then drawn to art who by their mental constitution were admirably fitted to be pure scientists. The creative energy of these Renaissance Italians, and it was immense, was channelled into the arts; and directly from art there opened up the fields of mathematics and science.

The completion of Florence's cathedral by Brunelleschi, with his daring conception of covering a crossing of 138 feet in diameter by an octagonal drum and pointed dome, marked the triumphant acceptance of the constructional principles of Renaissance architecture. When, in 1420, the plan for the dome was agreed to, Brunelleschi was already engaged on the charming little Pazzi Chapel (with its façade designed as a prostyle Roman temple) in the cloisters of S. Croce. His other work in Florence included the churches of S. Spirito and of S. Lorenzo, whose Corinthian columns supporting entablature-blocks were another classical revival. The huge Pitti Palace was later constructed to Brunelleschi's plans, with additions by Ammanati. L. B. Alberti, who has been seen as the prototype of the 'universal man' of the Renaissance, designed the Palazzo

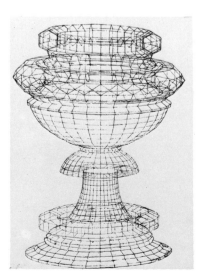

Left: Drawing of a chalice by Uccello (*c.* 1396–1474).

Right: Leonardo da Vinci, scientist and artist. A drawing of a flower ('The Star of Bethlehem') and a sketch for a tank.

Rucellai (1451) and the façade of S. Maria Novella in Florence, the church of S. Andrea in Mantua, and the unfinished Malatesta *tempio* of S. Francesco at Rimini, where he was assisted by Agostino di Duccio.

Of the Florentine palaces, the Palazzo Medici-Riccardi (1430) was built to the plans of Michelozzo, the friend of Cosimo de' Medici; and perhaps the most perfect, the Palazzo Strozzi, was begun in 1489 by Benedetto da Maiano and completed by Il Cronaca (Simone Pollaiuolo). Bramante (1444–1514), a native of Urbino, was first a painter; as an architect he gained prominence in Milan with the boldly conceived church of S. Satiro (1474). However, he is best known for his work in Rome, where he designed many palaces and churches (among them the Tempietto in S. Pietro in Montorio, the Palazzo della Cancelleria and the Belvedere Court in the Vatican), before Pope Julius II in 1505 appointed him, on Michelangelo's advice, as architect for the rebuilding of St Peter's. Bramante's pupils included Peruzzi, Sangallo, Raphael and Giulio Romano.

Consolidation of States and the Balance of Power

The extraordinary artistic and intellectual activity in the fifteenth century took place against a background of important changes in the conditions of the Italian despotisms, wherein the despots strove to promote the interests of the more productive sections of their subjects (and thereby an increase in their own revenues) by further restricting the influence of the nobles and by freeing the people from military service. Moreover, they sought to achieve the internal stability of accepted dynasties. By the Treaty of Lodi (1454) an attempt was made to establish a balance of power between five of the most prominent Italian states: Naples, Milan, Venice, Florence and the papacy. The smaller states, such as Ferrara, Urbino and Mantua, managed to survive by a judicious calculation of political moves; hence the skilful development of particularly Italian forms of statecraft, which found their outward expression in the art of diplomacy, in which practice Italy led the rest of Europe.

It was in the service of these princely courts that there now appeared a new class of professional man highly characteristic of the age – the humanist. The revival of the study of Latin and (henceforth increasingly) of Greek classics took place in a setting that was predominantly secular; fifteenth-century Italians looked at the world, and at themselves as part of it, no longer with a view to their eternal survival, but with the aim of understanding and enjoying life for its own sake. The Commercial Revolution had presented them with the material means

Above: Section-elevation, showing
Brunelleschi's dome for the Cathedral
of Florence, Sta Maria del Fiore
(after 1420).

Right: Design made by Brunelleschi
in 1419, to demonstrate the feasibility
of his dome. This design secured for
Brunelleschi the appointment of sole
architect of the cupola.

of creating a new civilization; and this had been achieved in defiance of the ethical principles preached by the Church. What was required by the despots and rich patricians of the Italian states was a set of concepts, a language, an ideology (if that were possible), which expressed contemporary social reality and the place that they had usurped within it. These intellectual tools were provided by the humanists; their first textbooks were the classics, rediscovered and re-interpreted.

Milan   Under the rule of Gian Galeazzo Visconti (1378–1402; created duke in 1395) Milan became the most powerful state in Italy, its territories extending from the frontiers of Piedmont to Padua and the Trevisan March; south of the River Po Gian Galeazzo controlled the Via Emilia as far as Bologna; and to the south of the Apennines he brought under his *signoria*, or under that of his nominees, Lucca, Pisa, Piombino, Siena, Perugia, Assisi and Spoleto, thus cutting off Florence from direct access to the sea and to Rome. It was typical of the man that

Gian Galeazzo Visconti presenting a model of his Certosa of Pavia to the Virgin. From a fresco by Ambrogio Borgognone, *c.* 1488.

A lecture at the Montefeltro court of Urbino before Duke Federigo and the young
Guidoballo. Attributed to Justus van Ghent.

he had gained power by outwitting and seizing his uncle Bernabò, the ruler of
Milan, and his family. No soldier, Gian Galeazzo consolidated his rule from his
study by the use of Milanese gold, which procured him the best mercenaries. For
hard cash he bought his first wife, the daughter of King John of France; a
husband, Louis d'Orléans, for his daughter Valentina (a marriage which later
gave rise to French claims on Milan); and his own title from the Emperor. Yet he
was a great patron of letters and the arts; it was he who began the construction of
the Cathedral of Milan (1386) and the beautiful Certosa of Pavia (1396). He
summoned the most eminent scholars to teach at the University of Pavia and
possessed a fine library. His ambitions were without limit and they might have led
him far, had not he been struck down by the plague, when he had set his mind to
the subjugation of Florence (1402).

His son, the last male Visconti, Filippo Maria, attempted without much
success to pursue his father's policy of territorial aggrandizement. On his death
in 1447 the ephemeral 'Ambrosian Republic' was proclaimed. The condottiere Francesco Sforza, who had married Bianca Maria, the illegitimate daughter
of Filippo Maria, calculating correctly the weakness of the republic, effected a
coup de main and was offered the *signoria*, assuming the title of duke of Milan

103

Francesco Sforza, Duke of Milan;
a portrait by Francesco Bonsignore.
Sforza's court became one of the
most splendid in Italy.

(1450). Sforza was supported in his aspirations by the money and advice of
Cosimo de' Medici.

In the Sforza dukes of Milan we observe the tendencies already noted among
the Italian despots: all their actions were governed by their awareness of the
insecurity of their tenure. Francesco, the untutored Romagnol soldier, showed
the greatest respect for education: he had his children brought up in strict
accordance with the beliefs of the humanists; a scholar was imported from
Constantinople specifically to teach them Greek. Court life was of the utmost
brilliance. The Sforzas were indefatigable builders: vast irrigation works were
carried out; streets and piazzas were widened and embellished; work was
begun on the Castello and on the beautiful Ospedale Maggiore, to the designs
of the Florentine Filarete (d. 1465).

After the death of Francesco's son, the odious Galeazzo Maria (1466–76),
who was assassinated, the power in Milan was gathered into the hands of his
brother Lodovico 'il Moro', a man who summed up in his own person the
exceptional qualities required of the Renaissance prince. The court of Milan,
presided over by Lodovico and his gifted young wife Beatrice d'Este, who
overshadowed the rightful duke, Gian Galeazzo, and his wife Isabella of
Naples, was the goal for men of talent and imagination in search of employment
– men such as Bramante and, towering above them all, Leonardo da Vinci.

In January 1377 Pope Gregory XI, responding to the appeals of Italians voiced with such conviction by the *popolana* Caterina Benincasa (St Catherine of Siena, 1347–80), returned to Rome from the 'Babylonian Captivity'. He died in the following year and the conclave of sixteen cardinals, of whom only four were Italian, elected Bartolomeo Prignano, archbishop of Bari, who took the name of Urban VI (1378–89). The election was perfectly regular, although the Roman crowds had been turbulent in their demand for an Italian Pope. Nevertheless, the twelve foreign cardinals met again at Anagni, declared Urban a usurper chosen under duress and elected the notorious Robert, bishop of Cambrai (Clement VII, 1378–94), to the 'vacant' see. Thus began the Great Schism, with the simultaneous existence of two Popes, one residing in Rome and the other in Avignon, a state of affairs which was not healed until the Council of Constance in 1414–16, when a Roman Colonna was unanimously elected Martin V (1417–31). This council established the principle of what was known as the Conciliar Movement, whereby the general councils of the Church were held to be superior to the papacy. Pope Eugenius V (1431–47), however, reasserted the claims of the papacy against its opponents at the Council of Basle and the movement died.

In the person of Nicholas V (1447–55) one of the most cultivated humanists of the age occupied the papal throne. With the intention of restoring the ancient

Lodovico Sforza ('il Moro', 1451–1508) usurped the Duchy from his nephew Gian Galeazzo (left) in 1481.

Pope Gregory XI on his return to Rome from the 'Babylonian Captivity' at Avignon, 1377. From a painting by Giorgio Vasari, who wrote the celebrated *Lives* of artists.

grandeur of his capital, Nicholas employed the Florentines Alberti and Rossellino as his architects and Fra Angelico, Benozzo Gozzoli and Piero della Francesca as painters. An avid collector of manuscripts all his life, Nicholas left at his death some nine thousand volumes, which formed the nucleus of the Vatican Library. Humanists were employed as his secretaries, and no documents of state were permitted to appear unless written in elegant Latin and in a beautiful hand. But it was a humanist, Stefano Porcari, fired like Cola di Rienzo with classical zeal, who fomented an abortive conspiracy to restore the Roman republic (1453). This, and the fall of Constantinople to the Turks in the same year, saddened Nicholas's end. Pius II (1458–64) was as enthusiastic a humanist as Nicholas, and he was moreover a literary artist who in his *Commentaries* has left delightful pictures of the countryside and of the daily life of the period. During his pontificate the Roman Academy was founded by the humanist Julius Pomponius Laetus, and a bull was issued in order to protect the remaining monuments of ancient Rome from further deterioration. The publication of Flavio Biondo's (d. 1463) encyclopaedic work on Roman antiquities, *Roma instaurata, Roma triumphans* and *Italia illustrata*, initiated the scientific study of archaeology.

The elevation of Francesco della Rovere, a humbly born native of Savona, as Pope Sixtus IV (1471–84), ushered in a new era. Yet like his predecessor, Sixtus was a patron of artists and scholars; foremost among the latter was

The coronation of Robert of Cambrai as Clement VII (1378–90), simultaneously with the perfectly valid election of Pope Urban VI, began the 'Great Schism', ended only at the Council of Constance, 1416.

Pope Sixtus IV is depicted by Melozzo da Forlì appointing the humanist Platina as Librarian of the Vatican. With him are his della Rovere and Riario nephews.

Platina, whom he made librarian to the Vatican. It is to Sixtus that we owe the Sistine Chapel. The list of the artists he employed is impressive: Perugino, Signorelli, Ghirlandaio, Botticelli, Piero di Cosimo, Melozzo da Forlì, Pinturicchio and others. His policy was dictated by flagrant nepotism. His desire was to enrich his nephews: two, Pietro Riario and Giuliano della Rovere, were made cardinals; two others he provided with lordships of cities and with well connected wives. Sixtus, who was bitterly hostile to Lorenzo de' Medici for opposing these plans, was a party to the Pazzi Conspiracy against the Medici (1478); his wars against Florence and Ferrara were motivated rather for selfish ends than for reasons of state. His successor, Innocent VIII (1484–92), practised nepotism for the benefit of his natural sons; but his efforts were ineffectual in comparison with those of the Spaniard Roderigo Borgia, Alexander VI (1492–1503). Two of Alexander's qualities would have been admirable – in anybody but a Pope: the affection he bore his children and their mothers, and the administrative knowledge and skill which he used to serve their ends. The career of his son Cesare Borgia – who attempted, with his father's active support, to carve out a state for himself in central Italy and Romagna – was one of cold-blooded perfidy.

Pope Alexander VI.

Left: René I of Anjou, who succeeded Joanna II in 1435, was driven from his Kingdom of Naples by Alfonso, King of Aragon and Sicily, in 1442. *Right:* Sketch by Pisanello for a medal depicting Alfonso 'il Magnanimo', King of Naples, 1442–58.

The vacillations of the childless Queen Joanna II of Naples (1414–35) in appointing her heir left at her death two contestants in the field: René of Anjou and Alfonso, king of Aragon and Sicily. Alfonso had been captured by the Genoese and imprisoned in Milan: but he persuaded Filippo Maria Visconti (who had at first sided with René) that the presence of the French in Italy was dangerous, and that there were advantages in an alliance with himself. The French were then driven from the kingdom, and Alfonso ceremoniously entered Naples on 2 June 1442.

The Kingdom of Naples

To his contemporaries Alfonso was known as 'il Magnanimo', from the liberality with which he rewarded the humanists and artists who thronged his court. In his service were the Greek scholars George of Trebizond and the younger Chrysoloras, the historians Panormita and Bartolomeo Facio; his secretary, the scholar and poet Gioviano Pontano, was ennobled and liberally rewarded. Also employed by him were the Roman-born Lorenzo Valla, whose erudition and critical acumen were used mainly against the Church (he exposed the forgery of the *Donation of Constantine*), and the exiled Florentine humanist and governor Gianozzo Mannetti. Apart from these classical interests Alfonso was well versed in theology; nor were his aesthetic tastes restricted to antiquity, for he was a connoisseur of contemporary painting and the proud possessor of some Van Eycks. Alfonso's humanist passion was not shared by his illegitimate son, Ferrante, who succeeded him in 1458. The dissatisfaction of the nobles of the kingdom, led by Antonio Sanseverino, prince of Salerno, in concert with Innocent VIII and the Angevin pretender, René of Lorraine, came to a head in the Barons' Conspiracy (1485), which was crushed with treacherous cruelty by Ferrante. Such methods of political coercion, by no means uncommon, show the reverse side of the culture of the Renaissance.

Venice The geographical position of Venice and, more expressly, the intensely practical – commercial, naval and political – nature of the occupations of its citizens, delayed the arrival of the Renaissance in that city. The conspiracy of Baiamonte Tiepolo (1310) against the aristocratic government had led to the institution of the Council of Ten, and this body was effective in suppressing a second conspiracy, that of the Doge Marino Faliero, which resulted in his execution (1355). In 1378 the long-standing maritime rivalry between Venice and Genoa

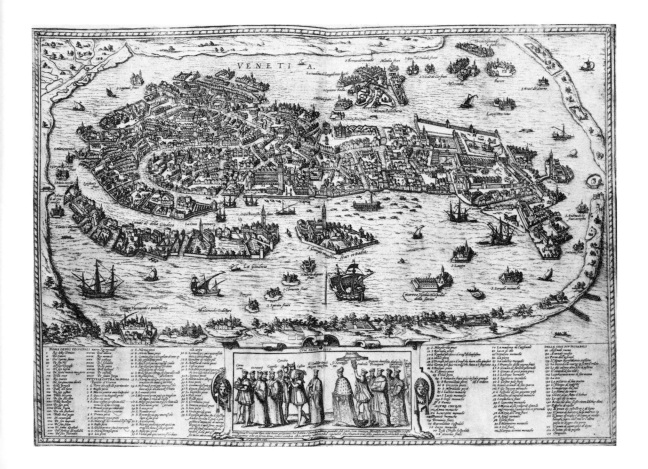

The Doge of Venice with members of the Great Council. From a sketch attributed to Antonio Veregiano.

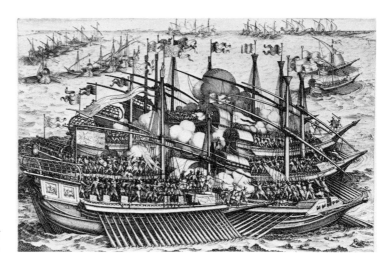

Naval battle between ships manned by the Knights of Malta and the Moslems.

erupted in war; the capture of Chioggia by the Genoese threatened the very existence of the Venetian republic, until the combined fleets of Vittor Pisani and Carlo Zeno succeeded in turning the tables on the Genoese and forcing them to capitulate (1380). The Doge Tommaso Mocenigo, who died in 1423, advocated a policy of concentrating on Venice's eastern empire and sea-power, and of refusing to be drawn into a struggle with Milan for the *terraferma*. His successor, Francesco Foscari (1423–57), reversed this policy. In the wars which followed the condottiere Carmagnola was suspected by the Venetians of sacrificing their interests to those of his former employer Filippo Maria Visconti; recalled to Venice, he was tortured into confession, and beheaded

111

◀ Venice in 1572, from *Civitates orbis terrarum*, by G. Braun and F. Hogenberg.

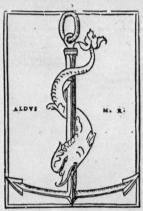

The *editio princeps* of the works of the Greek grammarian Athenaeus (*fl.* end of second and beginning of third century). Published by Aldus Manutius in 1514.

(1432). Venetian gains on the mainland reached their final limits in the former territories of Brescia and Bergamo. In 1453 the Venetians received the shock of the fall of Constantinople; four years later they witnessed the humiliation and deposition of the luckless Foscari. The commercial aristocracy had secured its supremacy; but in quality this period saw the beginning of the long decline.

Venice was at first an intermediary rather than an instigator in the revival of Greek letters. When the scholar Manuele Chrysoloras arrived in Venice in 1396 on a diplomatic mission from the Eastern Emperor Manuel II, who was seeking Italian aid against the Turks, it was not the Venetians but the Florentines who saw the advantage of securing his services as professor of Greek in their own university. Guarino da Verona (1374–1460), finding employment with a Venetian merchant, visited Constantinople in 1403; and there he studied for two years under Giovanni Chrysoloras, Manuele's brother, returning with a number of codices. He afterwards set up a school for Venetian nobles, where he had as a pupil his friend Vittorino de Feltre, the second of the great Renaissance educators. Another enthusiastic Hellenist, Giovanni Aurispa, arrived in Venice from Constantinople in 1423 with no fewer than 238 rare volumes. In 1433, during his exile, Cosimo de' Medici presented to the city the nucleus of the library of S. Giorgio Maggiore. In 1468 the Greek scholar and patron of scholars, Cardinal Bessarion, left to St Mark's his library of six hundred Greek and Latin manuscripts; yet with characteristic apathy to the classical revival the Venetians long neglected to provide it with adequate housing.

At the end of the century, however, Venice to some extent made amends for the tardiness of her contribution to the renaissance of learning. In 1490 Aldo Manuzio, a native of Padua, established his printing house in Venice and gave to a world eager for the possession of books the splendid Aldine octavo editions of classical texts. The first Italian press had been set up at Subiaco in 1465 by the Germans Schweinheim and Pannartz. The Italians, with their cultivated sense of style, made great progress in the production of elegant and accurately edited books. The Roman type was perfected in Venice, and it is to Aldo Manuzio that we owe the cursive Italic script, said to have been based on Petrarch's handwriting. The typography of the Greek texts was equally clear and well formed. Aldo's work was carried on after his death in 1515 by members of his family and a body of scholarly editors. The appearance of the Aldine books, with their famous sign of the dolphin and anchor, marked a stage in the wider diffusion of classical knowledge.

From a combination of causes impossible adequately to evaluate, the history of *Florence* the Renaissance in the fourteenth and fifteenth centuries is virtually the history of Florence: other cities made their contribution to the general culture, but in none did the intense quality of its civic life produce such a variety of splendid achievement. For a great part of the fourteenth century the power in Florence was at the disposal of the caucus of the Parte Guelfa, which consisted of heads of patrician clans under the leadership of the Albizzi. Opposed to them were the Ricci, Alberti and Medici families, who found support among the lower classes. A proletarian uprising, the revolt of the Ciompi (wool-carders) in 1378, resulted in the appointment of the wool-carder Michele di Lando as gonfalonier of justice. But the Parte Guelfa succeeded in regaining supremacy three years later. Their opponents were exiled or excluded from office ('admonished') and from that time until 1434 Florence was ruled by Maso degli Albizzi, followed by his son Rinaldo.

This period brought an extension of Florentine territory by the acquisition of Arezzo, Pisa, Cortona, Leghorn and Montepulciano; it was also marked by the consolidation of the influence of the Medici in civic affairs. Using the enormous wealth gained in their banking business – they were papal bankers and had branches in sixteen European cities – the Medici aimed at the leadership of the party in opposition to the Albizzi. In 1433 Rinaldo secured the banishment of Cosimo de' Medici (1389–1464), but in the succeeding year, the *signoria* being favourable to the Medici, Cosimo was recalled in triumph; there followed a proscription of his enemies, with the confiscation of their property, and thenceforth Cosimo became the effective ruler of Florence. The outward form of the

The Medici family as the Magi. From a painting (*c.* 1459) by Benozzo Gozzoli in the Medici Palace, Florence.

View of Florence, *c.* 1495, dominated by Brunelleschi's cupola of Sta Maria del Fiore.
To the left can be seen the tower of the Palazzo Vecchio.

republic was maintained, the Medicean party governing by a manipulation of the elections and by the device of appointing commissions with extraordinary powers (*balíe*).

Serious and unassuming in manner, Cosimo combined a shrewd grasp of practical affairs and a knowledge of men with a deep understanding of the arts and letters. He was a magnificent patron; his subtle eye for talent, his appreciation of a work of art and his tact in dealing with artists drew the best from the architects, sculptors and painters in his service – such men as Alberti, Brunelleschi, Michelozzo, Ghiberti, Donatello, Fra Angelico, Filippo Lippi and Benozzo Gozzoli. The Palazzo Medici (now Riccardi), the Convent of S. Marco, the Badia (abbey) at Fiesole, the church of S. Lorenzo, and his villas at Careggi and Caffagiuolo bear witness to his taste. He was an assiduous collector of codices and books, employing for this purpose the learned bookseller Vespasiano Bisticci, whom he appointed his librarian. In 1439 Pope Eugenius

Cosimo de' Medici,
'Pater Patriae'
(d. 1464).

115

Coronation of the Emperor Sigismund by Pope Eugenius IV during the Council of the Eastern and Western Churches, held in Florence in 1439. Bronze panel from a door of St Peter's, Rome.

IV, an exile from Rome, held a council in Florence, attended by the Eastern Emperor John VII (Palaeologos) and the patriarch of Constantinople, with the aim of reuniting the Greek and Latin Churches. Among the Greeks of learning present were the Platonist scholars Gemistos Plethon and (the later Cardinal) Bessarion. Their visit encouraged the study of Greek and led Cosimo to found the Platonic Academy, which was later presided over by his protégé Marsilio Ficino, the translator and expounder of Plato.

Florence was well served by a series of men of letters who occupied the positions of secretary or chancellor, among them Coluccio Salutati (d. 1406), an ardent collector of Greek codices and one of those responsible for bringing Chrysoloras to Florence, and Leonardo Bruni (d. 1444), who wrote the city's history. Niccolò Niccoli (d. 1437) abandoned mercantile pursuits in order to form a library of Greek and Latin texts (which he edited and copied with his own hand), as well as a valuable collection of ancient works of art. On his death his art treasures were absorbed in the Medici collection, and his books formed the beginning of the Laurentian Library (*Biblioteca Laurenziana*). It was Cosimo who secured for his city the best Hellenist of the day, Giovanni Argyropoulus, a refugee from Constantinople, who was appointed to the chair of Greek, which he held from 1456 to 1471, thereby ensuring Florence's preeminence in Greek studies. To his lectures came a generation of remarkable men, which included Poliziano, Pico della Mirandola and Lorenzo de' Medici.

On the death of Cosimo, 'Pater Patriae', in 1464 his role as unofficial prince was filled by his ailing son Piero, who survived him only five years. When

Terracotta bust of Lorenzo il Magnifico. Usually attributed to Verrocchio, but possibly executed from a death-mask by one of his pupils.

Medal (obverse and, *below*, reverse) depicting the humanist Marsilio Ficino. Attributed to Niccolò Fiorentino (before 1500).

Piero died a deputation of citizens called on his sons Lorenzo and Giuliano, asking them to occupy the place held by their father and grandfather. The reign of Lorenzo il Magnifico (1469–92) – for the pretences of political liberty could be no longer sustained, after he had appointed a council of seventy as a form of permanent *balía*, which gathered all power into his hands – marked the meridian of the Renaissance in Florence.

The circle which surrounded Lorenzo in his *palazzi*, gardens or country villas was of great brilliance. The almost idolatrous respect paid to Platonic (or Neoplatonic) philosophy at the symposia of the Academy did not prevent a revival of the *volgare* in the poetry and prose of Alberti (*Della famiglia*), Poliziano (*Orfeo, Rispetti*), Pico della Mirandola, Lorenzo de' Medici (*Nencia da Barbarino, Canzoni, Canti Carnascialeschi*) and Luigi Pulci (*Morgante Maggiore*). Botticelli's *Primavera* and the *Birth of Venus* might have been painted as illustrations for Poliziano's *Stanze per la giostra*, written in honour of Giuliano de' Medici. Lorenzo added greatly to the Medicean collections of antiquities, painting, sculpture and books. It was in his gardens by the side of St Mark's that the young Michelangelo worked under Bertoldo, Donatello's pupil.

The painters most favoured by Lorenzo were Botticelli, Ghirlandaio and Benozzo Gozzoli. He encouraged the young Leonardo da Vinci, but about 1483 the latter sought employment with Lodovico Sforza. Perhaps Leonardo found the Platonic theorizing of Lorenzo's circle too vapid; he preferred the company of mathematicians like Benedetto Aritmetico or the physician, geographer and astronomer Paolo Toscanelli. Lorenzo's closest associates, after the assassination of Giuliano (1478) at the hands of the Pazzi, were mostly scholars, poets, artists, wits and members of the Platonic Academy: Landino, Ficino, Poliziano, Pulci and Pico della Mirandola.

The fairer aspects of Lorenzo's character come out in the patronage and companionship of such men; but he was ruthless in the pursuit of his ends, as is seen by his treatment of the Pazzi, the sack of Volterra, and the robbing of the dowry money of the poor. On his return from the dangerous and successful mission to King Ferrante of Naples (1479), the signs of despotism were apparent. Nevertheless, the fruits of the reversal of his policy of a balance of power among the Italian states and the exclusion of foreign influence were clear two years after his death in 1492, with the French invasion of Charles VIII and the expulsion of the Medici from Florence – events foretold by Savonarola. The aim of Lorenzo's policy was to prevent the dissensions between Milan and Naples from provoking a general war; and on the death of Sixtus IV, Florence entered into close relations with the papacy, Innocent VIII marrying his son to Lorenzo's daughter and giving the cardinal's hat to Lorenzo's second son Giovanni (later Pope Leo X) at the tender age of fourteen.

The Pazzi Conspiracy, Sunday, 26 April 1478. Commemorative medal by Bertoldi di Giovanni, showing (*left*) Lorenzo and (*right*) his murdered brother Giuliano.

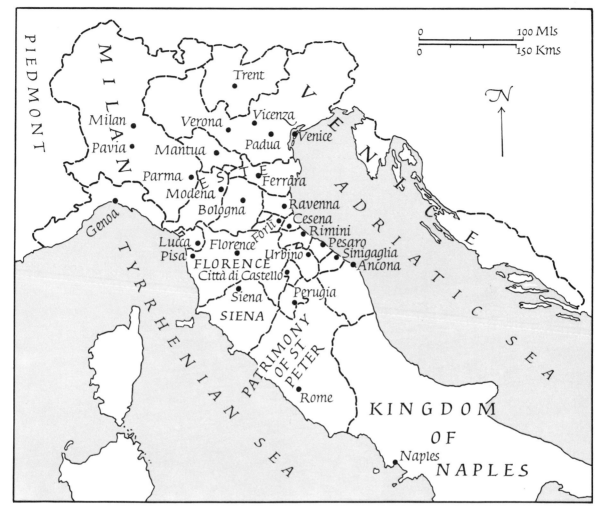

Italy at the time of the French invasions, from 1494.

If the light of the Renaissance shone most brightly in fifteenth-century Florence, the smaller, more aristocratic courts of Urbino, Ferrara and Mantua each had a notable contribution to make to a civilization which placed the Italians foremost among the peoples of Europe. These three states had characteristics in common: their territories were small, their survival was precarious among greater states which attempted to absorb them, and their rulers usually adopted the profession of condottiere – in fact, the military services rendered by the prince were often the principal source of state income.

The Smaller Courts

119

Of these princely families the Estensi were the most ancient. Azzo VI, marquis of Este, the first lord of Ferrara, died in 1212. Some two hundred years later, in 1429, Niccolò III, who had extended his power over Modena and Reggio, called to his court the humanist Guarino da Verona to educate his sons. Guarino's method of education, like that of his friend Vittorino da Feltre, was based on the maxims of Quintilian (*De institutione oratoria*) and was profoundly influenced by Christian principles. Latin and Greek were the mainstay of his system and his pupils were widely read in classical literature; other subjects included history, mathematics, astronomy and natural history. Nor was physical development neglected; games, gymnastics, dancing, swimming, riding and excursions in the countryside filled the intervals from study. The living was spare, but the pupils' quarters were pleasant; and everything was directed towards an ease and elegance of manner and deportment. No corporal punishment was allowed, and where possible teaching was carried out through play. The leading families of Italy and other countries sent their sons to Guarino's and Vittorino's schools; beside them, and sharing in all their activities, were a number of poor but promising boys, who were kept at the masters' expense. Such was their success in later life that this revolutionary system of education

Above: The famous humanist schoolmaster, Guarino da Verona (1374–1460).

Right: Orlando Furioso, by Ariosto. The title-page, with the dedication to Hippolito d'Este, 1542.

Renaissance faience. Coloured plate, part of a
service bearing the arms of Gianfrancesco
Gonzaga, Marquis of Mantua, and of his
wife, Isabella d'Este.

became widely adopted. Leonello, Niccolò's successor, corresponded with the
leading humanists of the day and it was he who inspired Alberti to write his
book on architecture, *De re aedificatoria*.

The Este brothers Leonello, Borso and Ercole took great pleasure in the
building of villas and palaces (Belfiore, Schifanoia, Belriguardo) and in the
laying out of gardens. Pisanello, Piero della Francesca, Cosimo Tura, Francesco della Cossa, Ercole de' Roberti were among the painters employed
by the Estensi in decorating the rooms which held their collections of art treasures and the magnificent library. All these princes delighted in the gorgeous
display of processions and the theatre. Boiardo was the court poet and it was in
Ferrara that he wrote *Orlando Innamorato*, which was continued some years later
by Ariosto in his *Orlando Furioso*. The court of Ferrara was famed for its theatre
and its music, the ducal family (Borso was created duke in 1490) being skilled
instrumentalists. The equality of the sexes, which was so distinguished a feature
of the Renaissance in Italy, was carried further in Ferrara than in other cities;
there the social freedom of women was extended to girls.

Borso's brother Ercole (d. 1505) married Leonora of Aragon, daughter of
King Ferrante of Naples, who gave birth to two daughters, later in life to become
perhaps the most typical of the great ladies of the Renaissance: Isabella, who
married Gianfrancesco Gonzaga, marquis of Mantua, and Beatrice, who became the wife of Lodovico il Moro. The Gonzagas had been lords of Mantua
since 1328, when Luigi supplanted his brother-in-law Rinaldo Bonacolsi.

121

The traditions of the family were military, but Gianfrancesco I (d. 1407) had wider interests – besides collecting pictures and precious objects, he encouraged the manufacture of tapestries and cloth, trades which returned the state a steady income. It was his son, also a Gianfrancesco and a soldier, rewarded by the Emperor Sigismund with the title of marquis in 1432, who brought to Mantua Vittorino da Feltre to educate his family. In Vittorino's school, appropriately named *La Casa Gioiosa* (joyful house), the girls were instructed with the boys, and Cecilia Gonzaga was one of his favourite pupils. Thenceforth the Gonzagas were with the foremost in their patronage of the arts and letters and in the cultiva-tion of their court, which reached its highest point in the reign of Gianfrancesco III (1484–1519) and his wife Isabella d'Este.

Isabella was a somewhat rapacious collector; her gallery contained pictures by Mantegna (the court painter), Michelangelo, Leonardo da Vinci (a pastel now in the Louvre), Costa, Perugino, Correggio, Giovanni Bellini, Raphael and Titian. Her library was stocked with the choicest volumes, often presenta-tion copies, such as those of Boiardo, Ariosto and Trissino. Mantua had long been famous for its music and the marchioness imported Flemish, French and other foreign musicians practised in the *ars nova*. Poliziano's pastoral drama *Orfeo*, the ancestor of the opera, had been first produced in Mantua in 1471.

The family of Lodovico III Gonzaga ('il Turco', d. 1478), soldier and art patron, painted by his court painter, Mantegna.

Piero della Francesca's portrait of Federigo da Montefeltro, Duke of Urbino from 1444 until 1482, one of the most distinguished of Renaissance princes.

In 1489 Isabella's sister-in-law Elisabetta married Guidobaldo, the eldest son of the great Federigo, duke of Urbino (d. 1482). Educated in the humanities at the school of Vittorino da Feltre and instructed in the art of war by the condottieri Niccolò Piccinino and Francesco Sforza, Federigo, when free from military expeditions, devoted himself to the prosperity of his tiny state – to the building of churches, monasteries, hospitals and schools, the promotion of learning (particularly Greek), and the administration of justice. Alone of the princes of his time, he would walk unattended through the city, conversing with all. The court of Urbino was the school for the nobility of Italy. Federigo's memorial survives in his magnificent palace constructed by Luciano Laurana, but for much of which Federigo was his own architect. Yet his greatest source of pride was his library, which is said to have cost him 30,000 ducats, the volumes, bound in crimson ornamented with silver, all being copied in a beautiful hand – he would not deign to possess a printed book. Perhaps the greatest commemoration of the splendid civilization of Urbino is found in the pages of *Il Cortegiano*, where Baldassare Castiglione pays his tribute to the court of Federigo's son Guidobaldo and his wife Elisabetta Gonzaga.

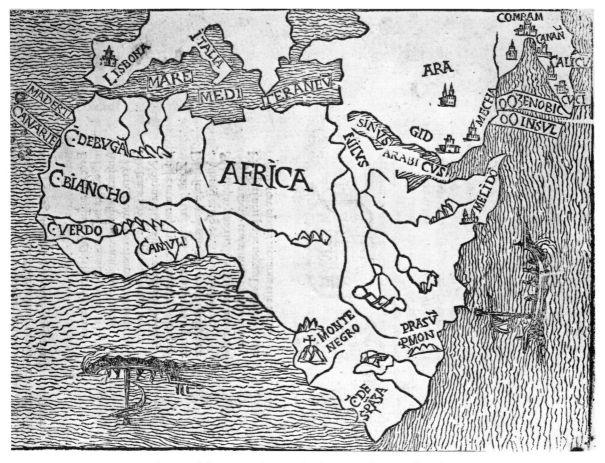

The age of discovery. Significantly, this map of 1508 is from the *Itinerarium Portugallensium*.

Chapter Six

THE NEW BARBARIANS, 1494–1796

The Florentine historian and statesman Guicciardini, looking back from the aftermath of the French invasions, recalled the state of Italy in about the year 1490: 'Italy had never experienced such prosperity. . . . Everywhere the country enjoyed profound peace and tranquility.' For more than three centuries, through the Commercial Revolution and its cultural sequel the Renaissance, Italy had led Europe in commerce, industry and the arts of civilization; then at the end of the fifteenth century this primacy passed from her. The very brilliance of her achievements left her exposed to the cupidity of nations less civilized but politically more compact and more disposed to military discipline.

Three factors may be taken into account in considering this reversal of roles between Italy and the northern nations. Firstly, her geographical position no longer uniquely favoured her. After the capture of Constantinople by the Ottoman Turks in 1453 there was a continual threat to her traffic with the East; it was increasingly those nations placed propitiously on the Atlantic seaboard that took up the challenge of finding new trade routes to the Orient.

Ironically, Italians contributed largely to these expeditions of discovery, whose fruits they were not to share. Some years before the Portuguese navigators Bartolomeo Diaz and Vasco da Gama opened the passage to India via the Cape of Good Hope, the Florentine physicist Paolo Toscanelli (d. 1482) had argued the possibility of reaching the Far East by sailing west, basing his hypothesis on the sphericity of the earth and on the vast extension of the Asian land-mass. It was acting on this theory that Christopher Columbus (1451–1506), a Genoese in the service of Spain, made three Atlantic voyages, discovering the West Indies and America (1492–1504). The Florentine Amerigo Vespucci, who undertook his voyages on behalf of Spain and Portugal, sailed along the coast of Venezuela ('Little Venice') and brought the American discoveries to the attention of Europe. Later the continents were named after him. Under the patronage of the English crown, John Cabot, a Genoese-born Venetian, and his son Sebastian, failing in their attempt to find a north-west passage to India, discovered Labrador and Hudson Bay (1497). Another Italian, Giovanni di Verazzano, in the employment of the king of France, made the discovery of the Gulf of St Lawrence. The re-routing of the passage to the East and the opening up of the New World profited the Atlantic countries, and broke the monopoly of the Italian seaports. Of equal significance with this shift in the commercial centre of gravity was the change brought about in men's mental attitudes by the discovery of rich and ancient civilizations, of new flora and fauna, and by the intellectual stimulus presented by distant navigation, which required the development of instruments, charts, maps and tables, and the observation and collection of astronomical data, all of which gave encouragement to the progress of pure and applied mathematics. Many useful additions were made to the pharmacopeia. These developments were general throughout Europe. Italian diet was profoundly affected, however, by the introduction of the tomato from Peru, the prickly pear (*fichi d'India*) and Mexican maize.

The second factor which contributed to Italy's weakness in relation to the strongly centralized monarchies of France, Spain and, to a lesser degree, of the Habsburgs, was political. The rulers of such consolidated states, and they alone, had at their disposal the financial resources necessary to provide siege artillery, at that time coming into general use, and to hire good infantry. Man for man, Italians were not militarily inferior to foreigners: at the famous Challenge of Barletta (1503) a body of Italians under Prospero and Fabrizio Colonna defeated in combat the champions of France; and the Italians also had commanders of skill and courage, such as the same Colonna or Giovanni de' Medici (delle Bande Nere). But their military failures against the French, Spaniards and Germans reflected their incapacity to take concerted action. There was a long tradition of recourse to foreign arms by Popes and cities in order to gain a temporary advantage over their political rivals. Alliances between Italian states were *ad hoc*; mutual distrust was ingrained, and, since civic loyalties alone were envisaged, inevitable. It was only a Machiavelli who could look further; and the remedies he proposed in *The Prince* were a measure of his diagnosis of the seriousness of Italy's political ills. When Machiavelli or Guicciardini spoke of 'Italy', they had in mind not so much a 'geographical expression', or even a racial and cultural homogeneity, as a political aspiration.

Giovanni delle Bande Nere (de' Medici, 1498–1526), the brilliant condottiere from whom the Medici ducal line in Tuscany descended.

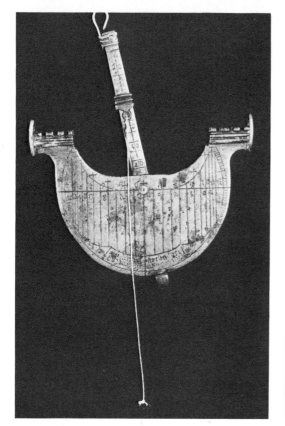

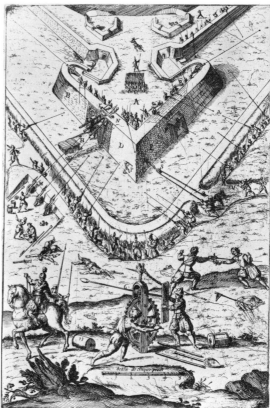

Left: Portable ship dial, known as the *Navicula de Venetiis*, 'the little ship of Venice' (*c.* 1450?). Allowances for latitude and for the time of year made possible a reading of the hour of the day. *Right:* Developments in fortification, designed to meet the needs of defence against the improved artillery of the period.

In 1494 the internal balance of power fostered by Lorenzo il Magnifico was permanently shattered by the invasion of Charles VIII of France, who revived the claims of the house of Anjou to the Aragonese kingdom of Naples. The ease with which he gained his object was not lost on others: for three centuries Italy was to remain defenceless before a succession of barbarian invaders; and it was no compensation for her loss that in the course of these centuries her civilization was to spread throughout Europe.

The immediate results of Charles's intervention in Italian affairs were the expulsion of the Medici from Florence, where the republic was restored under the guidance of Savonarola, and the rapid formation of a 'Holy League' against the French between Pope Alexander VI, Lodovico il Moro, the Venetians, Ferdinand and Isabella of Spain, and the Habsburg emperor. The League's army, but for the incompetence of its commander, the marquis of Mantua,

The entry of King Charles VIII of France into Florence on 17 November 1494. From the painting by Francesco Granacci (1477–1543).

might have destroyed the French forces, as they retreated northwards from Naples, at the inconclusive battle of Fornovo. Louis XII, who succeeded Charles in 1498, claimed both the throne of the Two Sicilies and, as a descendant of Valentina Visconti, the duchy of Milan. He crossed into Italy in 1498. Lodo-vico il Moro was temporarily driven into exile. Ultimately dispossessed, he was sent as a prisoner to France, where he died. Louis then came to an agreement with Ferdinand of Spain for a joint conquest and partition of the Neapolitan kingdom; but the allies fell out over the division, and when the French were defeated by Gonzalo de Cordova on the River Garigliano (December 1503), the kingdom passed into the possession of Spain. With a Spanish viceroy in Naples and a French governor in Milan, the Italian states had lost effective control over their own affairs.

A further pointer to their political future was seen five years later, when by the formation of the League of Cambrai Venice was despoiled of her mainland territories at the battle of Agnadello (1509). After Agnadello Pope Julius, fearing French predominance in northern Italy, withdrew from the alliance,

Allegory of the War of the League of Cambrai. From a painting by Palma Giovani
(1544–1628) in the Doge's Palace, Venice.

formed another 'Holy League' with Venice (1511), and purchased the support
of 20,000 Swiss mercenaries to drive out the French – 'Away with the barbarians!' The League was at first frustrated by the brilliance of the young French
general, Gaston de Foix, until his death in the moment of victory at the battle of
Ravenna (April 1512) left the French leaderless, with the result that they were
forced to retire beyond the Alps. Florence, where the republican government
had conferred the office of gonfalonier for life on Pier Soderini, had refused to
join the allies. The army of the League now marched on Prato, put to flight
the citizen levies raised by Machiavelli and committed such atrocities against
the inhabitants that Florence quickly surrendered. The Medicean government
was restored under Cardinal Giovanni, son of Lorenzo il Magnifico.

Francis I, who succeeded to the French throne in 1515, was determined to
recover Milan, which he achieved at the hard-fought battle of Marignano in
the same year. The election of the young Habsburg king of Spain as the Emperor
Charles V in 1519 was the beginning of a prolonged and bitter rivalry with
Francis I, which was fought out largely in northern Italy. The Medici Pope

Clement VII (1523–34) was nominally in alliance with the Emperor, but fearful of Francis's successes in Milan, he sought to insure his position by entering into secret negotiations with the French king. The destruction of the French forces and the capture of Francis by the imperial troops under the marquis of Pescara at Pavia (1525) radically altered the political balance in Italy. Yet in the following year Clement joined an alliance in support of the French. The result of this incompetent diplomacy was that an unpaid army of Lutheran *Landsknechte*, Spaniards and Italians marched on Rome under the constable of Bourbon and put it to the sack with indescribable brutality (1527). Clement had no alternative but to seek a humiliating accommodation with the Emperor.

The political settlement between Charles V and Clement at Bologna (1529–30) revealed in all its clarity the collapse of Italian independence with the Spanish in possession of Milan, Naples and Sicily and paramount throughout the peninsula. One further act proved this last point. Florence had expelled the Medici at the time of the sack of Rome. At Bologna Clement successfully sought the aid of imperial troops against the city. During a ten-month siege, its fortifications were superintended by Michelangelo, and the Florentine troops under Francesco Ferrucci showed that, when well led, they were superior to the enemy. It was the treachery of the mercenary captain Malatesta Baglione of Perugia which resulted in the city's capitulation (12 August 1530). With the overthrow of the republican government the absolute *signoria* was conferred on

Left: Papal Bull, setting out the heresies of Martin Luther. Rome, 1521. *Right:* A Lutheran caricature against the Pope: 'Gorgoneum Caput', *c.* 1577.

Alessandro de' Medici, the bastard son of Lorenzo, duke of Urbino, who was proclaimed hereditary duke (1532). This settlement of Italian affairs by Emperor and Pope lasted in its main features until after the wars of Louis XIV, when Spanish hegemony in the peninsula passed to the Austrians. From the coming of Charles VIII to the final restoration of the Medici in Florence thirty-six years of continual warfare had brought destruction to Renaissance Rome and devastation to some of the richest provinces of Italy.

A third factor in the decline of Italy from her earlier position of leadership among the European nations was a religious one. Outwardly a succession of strong Renaissance Popes had raised the papacy to unparalleled heights of ostentatious splendour and material power. Yet there had been repeated, if not always disinterested, calls for the reformation of the Church in head and members. It seemed implausible that the head (the Pope and the Curia) would remedy itself, which would require nothing less than conciliar intervention. Even a strong Pope, and one not guilty of nepotism, like Julius II, had reasons to fear a council convoked by his political opponents.

131

◄ The Sack of Rome, 1527. Pope Clement VII (de' Medici) held prisoner in the Castel Sant'Angelo by troops of the Emperor Charles V.

A painting by an unknown sixteenth-century Florentine artist, showing the burning of Savonarola and his companions in the Piazza della Signoria on 23 May 1498.

The Popes of the period were first and foremost 'political'. Religion and politics were inextricably enmeshed. The failure of such a deeply religious man as Savonarola in his quarrel with Alexander VI was essentially political. He could not maintain his hold over the imagination of the Florentines in face of the papal interdicts; he would have done well to remember Cosimo de' Medici's cynical truth that you cannot govern a state by paternosters. Both men were engaged in politics and in this art Alexander was incontestably the superior; Savonarola paid for his temerity with his life.

In 1517 the theological significance of Martin Luther's attack on indulgences at Wittenberg was lost on Pope Leo X; yet by mid-century most of Europe had broken free from direct papal control to constitute national Churches, headed by the monarch, either with a concordat regulating its relations with Rome, or else entirely autonomous, with its own form of Protestant doctrine and worship. Seemingly bereft of its political power, the papacy, under a series of reforming Popes, proceeded by slow steps to rectify the most obvious abuses and to instil a

A session of the Council of Trent (1543–63).

new, rather puritan spirit. In 1542 Pope Paul III revived the Inquisition, setting up the Holy Office under the ruthless zealot Carafa, who later, in 1559, as Pope Paul IV, promulgated the *Index Librorum Prohibitorum*.

The Popes were pressed by the Emperor Charles V to convene a council in order to effect a reconciliation between Catholics and Protestants, whose divisions were a threat to Habsburg rule. Yet the Council of Trent (1545–63) formulated matters of doctrine in a sense favourable to the Curia, but such that they made the division of Christendom henceforth irrevocable. Ecclesiastically, however, the Church benefited greatly by the Counter-Reformation; and the new spirit which informed it was shown in the foundation of further religious Orders, of which the most important, as the exponent of Catholic orthodoxy, was the Society of Jesus, founded by the Spaniard St Ignatius Loyola in 1540. The papacy of the Renaissance was replaced, externally at least, by an ecclesiastically minded Curia, dogmatic, devout, conformist – or, as its opponents would have it, obscurantist and hypocritical.

Drawing, attributed to Sebastiano del Piombo (*c.* 1485–1547) of Leo X (de' Medici, Pope, 1513–21).

High Renaissance in the Arts During the pontificates of Julius II (della Rovere, 1503–13) and Leo X (de' Medici, 1513–21) the centre of Renaissance art and humanist culture was papal Rome. There in the Vatican *Stanze* Raphael painted his *School of Athens* and the *Disputa*, perhaps the epitome of Renaissance ideals. Contemporaneously (1508–12) Michelangelo was engaged on the magnificent series of Old Testament scenes and majestic prophets and sibyls in the Sistine Chapel. A quarter of a century later he was to paint his *Last Judgment*, a work which reflects the profound change in society in the interval – the spiritual crisis brought about by the invasion and sack of Rome, by the collapse of humanist ideals and of a universal faith. In 1506 Pope Julius laid the foundation stone of the new St Peter's, designed by Bramante as a fitting symbol of the power and grandeur of the Catholic Church. St Peter's became the school for the diffusion of the architectural principles of the high Renaissance under a succession of notable architects, who followed Bramante and Raphael: Peruzzi, Giuliano da Sangallo, Michelangelo, Giacomo della Porta, Fontana and Vignola. At the beginning of the seventeenth century Maderna lengthened the nave and added the façade. Finally, in 1655–67 Bernini erected the stately piazza colonnade.

One of the typical Roman palaces of the Renaissance, the Palazzo Farnese, was partly the work of Michelangelo. Other examples of Michelangelo's architecture in Rome are the Capitoline piazza and S. Maria degli Angeli in the Baths of Diocletian; and in Florence the sacristy of S. Lorenzo and the Laurentian Library, built for Giulio de' Medici (Pope Clement VII). Giacomo Barozzi da Vignola (1507–73), the author of a treatise on the classical style (*Rule of the Five Orders of Architecture*), designed the Jesuit church of Il Gesù (1568); the existing façade, however, is by della Porta. The work of Pirro Ligorio (1510–83) is seen in the charming Villa Medici in Rome and the Villa d'Este at Tivoli, with its gardens and cascades. At the same period Galeazzo Alessi from Perugia was erecting splendid palaces for the rich noble families of Genoa. And in Mantua Giulio Romano (d. 1546) built for the Gonzaga the Palazzo del Tè, and at Bagnaia, in conjunction with Vignola, the beautiful casino and gardens of the Villa Lante.

Raphael Sanzio (1483–1520). Detail from 'The School of Athens', showing figures of Plato and Aristotle. Vatican.

Above: Jacopo Barozzi da Vignola. View of the interior of the church of Il Gesù, Rome, begun in 1568. *Below, left:* Exterior of Il Gesù. The façade is by Giacomo della Porta. *Below, right:* Church of Sta Maria della Salute, Venice, by Longhena (begun in 1632).

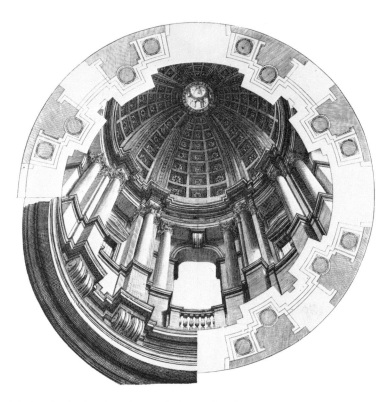

Above: Baroque architecture. Suggested design for the interior of a cupola, by Andrea Pozzo, 1693. *Below:* Andrea Palladio (1518–80). Villa Rotonda (Villa Capra), Vicenza, begun c. 1550.

Nor was Venice lacking in first-rate architects: Sansovino (a Florentine who fled there from the sack of Rome), Scamozzi, San Michele, and, somewhat later, Longhena (S. Maria della Salute, 1631). However, the most influential was Palladio of Vicenza (1508–80), the author of *The Four Books of Architecture*, who designed churches in Venice and the famous Villa Rotonda (Villa Capra) near Vicenza, as well as many other mainland villas. In Vicenza he built the Palazzo della Ragione (1549), a number of public buildings and private palaces, and in addition the celebrated Teatro Olimpico, which was begun in 1588 and completed after his death by Scamozzi.

In both Vignola's and Palladio's later work a change is to be observed from the classical to the mannerist style. This transition is most noticeable in Rome, where the striving after effect led from such incipient mannerist buildings, designed in reaction against Michelangelo, as Vignola's Il Gesù and the façade of the Villa Giulia to the fully fledged baroque of Gian Lorenzo Bernini (1598–1680; *baldacchino,* St Peter's, 1624; S. Andrea al Quirinale, 1658), Borromini (1599–1667; S. Carlo alle Quattro Fontane, 1638), Pietro da Cortona (1596–1669; S. Maria della Pace, 1656) and Filippo Juvarra (1676–1736; the Superga, Turin, 1717). The public works commissioned by Pope Sixtus V (1585–90; the Acqua Felice, the Via Sistina), and the construction of palaces, villas and gardens in the seventeenth century by the families of the 'grand nepotist' Popes, gave to Rome its characteristic baroque appearance. The city of Lecce in Apulia admirably illustrates today the divergent styles of Italian baroque architecture.

In sculpture and painting the influence of Michelangelo was decisive; but in the hands of lesser men there developed a mannerism which was often aesthetically degenerate. Important mannerist sculptors were Benvenuto Cellini (d. 1571), Sansovino (d. 1570), Ammanati (d. 1592), and the Flemish Giovanni di Bologna (d. 1608); masters of the succeeding baroque style were G. L. Bernini (notable for his fountains in Rome), Cosimo Fanzago (d. 1678) and Ferdinando Fuga (d. 1780), who is better known as an architect. The most celebrated of the earlier mannerist painters were Giulio Romano, who worked in Rome and Mantua (frescoes in the Palazzo del Tè), Rosso (d. 1540) and Pontormo (d. 1557) in Florence, and the influential Parmigianino (d. 1540) in Rome and Parma.

From mannerism stemmed two important movements in painting: the realist, whose greatest exponent was Caravaggio (1573–1610), and that of the eclectic school of the Carracci family (Ludovico, d. 1619; Agostino, d. 1602;

Parmigianino. Studies of nudes.

and Annibale, d. 1609) in Bologna, whose followers included Guido Reni (d. 1642), Domenichino (d. 1641) and Guercino (d. 1666). In Venice the Renaissance lived on, though not unaffected by these innovations, in the magnificent colourists, who derived much from Giorgione and the early Titian – Palma Vecchio (d. 1528), Sebastiano del Piombo (d. 1547), Bordone (d. 1571), Lorenzo Lotto (d. 1556) – and Venetian painting reached a glorious culmination in the late Titian (d. 1576, aged about ninety), Tintoretto (d. 1594) and Paolo Veronese (d. 1588).

With the two Florentines Niccolò Machiavelli (1469–1527) and Francesco Guicciardini (1483–1540), historical writing entered a new phase; so immensely superior were they to their predecessors, the chroniclers of emperors, Popes and cities (such as the Villani of Florence), that they launched a new literary form.

Literature

Medal by an unknown Bolognese artist (*c.* 1529) showing Francesco Guicciardini, statesman and historian.

Machiavelli sought from the comparison of events to draw general conclusions, vitiated at times by his undue reliance on Roman sources, but exercising a lasting influence on political thought, particularly by *The Prince*, whose subtlety of intention still perplexes scholars. Guicciardini, the practical statesman in the service of the Medici, is perhaps the better historian, combining as he does a clear vision of events with a deep understanding of human motivation (*Storia d'Italia, Ricordi*). Interest in biographical details of artists is shown by *The Lives of the Most Excellent Painters, Sculptors and Architects* of Giorgio Vasari (d. 1574). In prose the victory of Italian over Latin was consolidated by the publication of *Prose della volgar lingua* by the Venetian Cardinal Pietro Bembo (1470–1547); and Italian became increasingly adopted for historical, social and scientific works, gaining a fresh authority in the next century from the dialogues of Galileo Galilei. Among noteworthy prose writers of this period were Matteo Bandello (d. *c.*1560; the best novelist since Boccaccio), Pietro Aretino (d. 1556; a man of coarse spirit but of undeniable literary gifts), and Baldassare Castiglione (d. 1529; *Il Cortegiano*).

Between the deaths of Ariosto in 1533 and of Tasso in 1595 Italy produced a number of lyric poets, but, with the exception of Michelangelo, none was of the first rank: Bembo, Molza, Tansillo, Giovanni della Casa, Vittoria Colonna, Giulia Gonzaga, and another woman poet of distinction, Gaspara Stampa (1523–54) of Padua. Typical of the age was its taste for burlesque and satire: Berni, Aretino, Vinciguerra, and (in a different vein) Ariosto.

In the work of Torquato Tasso (b. 1544) the Renaissance had already succumbed to the enervating climate of the Counter-Reformation, yet his epic poem
Gerusalemme Liberata, however artificial in invention, emotion and style, is unique
in Italian literature, and is profoundly moving. Tasso also tried his hand at
pastoral drama in *Aminta* (1573), the precursor of the *Pastor Fido* of Guarini
(1590). Italian drama, both tragedy and comedy, was too closely modelled on
the ancients to produce much original work. Only in *La Calandria* by Bibbiena
(1513) did comedy begin to strike out afresh, and, with Grazzini (known as Il
Lasca), Cecchi, Ariosto, Aretino and Machiavelli, to seek its material in contemporary society. Machiavelli's *La Mandragora* (first performed in 1526) is a
comic masterpiece. Of indigenous growth, although its origins are obscure, was
the *commedia dell'arte*, a form of rude farce in local dialect, lending itself admirably
to satire. The bare framework of the plot (*scenario*) was given to the company
(Harlequin, Pulcinella, Brighella, Pantaloon, Zanies and others), who then
extemporized their parts. From the time of Pope Leo X the *commedia dell'arte*
became exceedingly popular with all classes, and Italian comedians were
acclaimed abroad.

Left: Galileo Galilei (1564–1642).
The title-page of his *Dialogo sopra
i due massimi sistemi del mondo.*

Right. The *commedia dell'arte.*
A Venetian figurine from Murano,
possibly representing the braggart
Spanish captain Mattamoros.

141

Music   Italy, with Ambrosian and Gregorian plainsong, was the home of church music. Early secular music was strongly influenced by French troubadours and trouvères. It is uncertain whether Guido d'Arezzo (fl. eleventh century), to whom is attributed the first attempt at a written notation, was in fact an Italian. The earliest known Italian composers of madrigals were Dante's friend Pietro Casella (d. before 1300) and Francesco Landini (c. 1325–97) of Florence; and this city was closely associated with the rise of the *ars nova*, music characterized by a newly developed freedom of rhythm and melody, and independence of vocal parts. For many years the Netherlands provided the majority of musicians for the papal court, and these included the great composers Dufay (d. 1474) and Josquin des Prés (d. 1521). A number of Flemish musicians held high positions in Italy. Among them were Willaert (d. 1562) at St Mark's, Venice; Arcadelt (d. 1575) at the Sistine Chapel, and Orlando di Lasso (d. 1594) at St John Lateran. These composers and teachers gave the impetus to the development of native Italian music.

Left: Woodcut title-page of book of lyrics by Lorenzo il Magnifico, Poliziano and others, including Lorenzo's 'Nencia da Barbarino', 1568. *Right:* Page from the score of Monteverdi's opera *L'Orfeo*, first performed in Mantua in 1607.

A professor of music, Francesco Gaffurio, lecturing on the theory and practice of music. The title-page of his book, Venice, 1512.

Palestrina (1525–94), also a composer of madrigals, reformed church music by purifying it of secular innovations and by raising its spiritual dignity and expressiveness in his great masses (such as *Missa Papae Marcelli*, 1562). Important composers of choral and instrumental music were the Venetians Gabrieli – the uncle Andrea (d. 1586), a pupil of Willaert, and his nephew Giovanni (d. 1612). In the last decade of the sixteenth century a group of humanist-minded *dilettanti* in Florence attempted to revive the Greek music of classical tragedy. The development of monody to convey action and feeling in recitative, in conjunction with the already advanced polyphony of the day, led to opera (*opera per musica*), Italy's latest outstanding contribution to Western art. In 1594 Peri (d. *c.* 1633) wrote *Daphne*, followed in 1600 by *Eurydice*, for which Caccini (d. *c.* 1615) supplied some sections and later reset the music. In the latter year Cavalieri produced in Rome the first oratorio for St Philip Neri's Oratory of the Divine Love – whence the name of the new form.

However, the most striking advances in musical expression were made by Claudio Monteverdi (1567–1643), whose profound originality is seen in his madrigals and his operas (*Orfeo*, Mantua, 1607; *L'Incoronazione di Poppea*, Venice, 1642). The aria was further developed by Cavalli (d. 1676) and by the prolific Alessandro Scarlatti (1660–1725), the founder of Neapolitan opera. With the aria came the school of *bel canto*, and later the tyranny of the singer. In 1537 was founded in Naples the first conservatory for instruction in music and singing, that of S. Maria di Loreto. The Neapolitan conservatories became

143

The Emperor Charles V. Detail from an equestrian portrait by Titian.

particularly famous through the teaching there of Scarlatti, Leo, Durante and Porpora. These schools spread the fame of Italian music throughout Europe, especially through the performances of the celebrated *castrati* singers: Caffarelli, Pacchierotti and, famous above all, Farinelli.

Spanish Supremacy On the death in 1535 of Francesco, the last of the house of Sforza, Milan was bestowed by the Emperor Charles V on his son Philip and his heirs. In 1540 Philip was proclaimed vicar-imperial in Italy, the Spanish rule being confirmed at the Peace of Cateau-Cambrésis (1559). Milan, Naples, Sicily, Sardinia and the Stato dei Presidi (on the Tuscan seaboard) now lay under Spanish suzerainty. But the pattern of political control in Italy was still a complicated one, with the duchy of Savoy under its ancient ruling house; the republic of Venice, with its mainland territories extending westwards to the River Adda, and also in control of the coasts of Istria and Dalmatia and the islands of Cyprus and Crete; the republic of Genoa, with Corsica; the duchy of Mantua, together with the territorially separate Montferrat, under the Gonzagas; the duchy of Parma and Piacenza under the Farnese (since 1545); the duchy of Ferrara, Modena and Reggio under the Estensi; Tuscany, with the exception of the republic of Lucca and the Stato dei Presidi, under Duke Cosimo de' Medici; and the Papal States.

144

View of the port and city of Palermo. ▶
From an eighteenth-century engraving.

With the final establishment of Spanish hegemony in the political sphere and of the papacy in the spiritual and increasingly in the intellectual, the fruitful (if at times chaotic) multiplicity and variety of Italian social life, the conditions which had placed Italy foremost in the development of Western civilization, were repressed under the sterile uniformity of foreign and absolutist governments. The main purpose of such representative bodies as the Spaniards permitted was to raise money to provide for the expenses of government, including the troops' pay and keep, and to supply the frequent *donativi* (gifts) to the Spanish throne.

In times of peace Milan was still rich enough to meet these demands. In the seventeenth century, however, Lombardy again became a battlefield between France, Spain and Austria, with the intermittent intervention of Savoy and Venice. In the Thirty Years War (1618–48) the struggle centred around the possession of the Valtellina. A disputed succession to Mantua and civil war in Savoy reopened hostilities, until the chief rivals, France and Spain, brought them temporarily to an end in the Peace of the Pyrenees (1659). In 1630 Mantua had been sacked by the Austrians and much of the precious art collections of Isabella Gonzaga destroyed or carried off. As a result of these wars and of the consequent financial exactions and restrictive trade policy of Spain, industry and agriculture in Lombardy seriously declined; famine and outbreaks of the plague (particularly that which followed the destruction of Mantua) added to the general misery. Many of the more prosperous classes emigrated to France or Venice. The condition of Sardinia under the Spaniards was equally ruinous.

In Sicily, as in Naples, the king of Spain was represented by the viceroy, nominally responsible to the distant Council of Italy at Madrid. The right of the Sicilian parliament (which consisted of three *brazos* or houses – the ecclesiastical,

Anonymous engraving, showing the plague of 1617 in Rome. The dead are being conveyed for burial.

baronial and domainial) to initiate legislation or present petitions had fallen into disuse. A standing committee, the Deputation, served to regulate the apportioning and collection of the *donativi*, which fell almost entirely on the poorest classes in the form of taxes (*gabelle*) on necessities. The economy of the island was exploited in the interest of Spain; in addition to the proceeds of taxation, large quantities of grain were exported to maintain Spanish armies in the almost constant continental wars. A succession of harvest failures led to revolts in Palermo, Girgenti (now Agrigento) and Catania in 1647. In Palermo the guilds of artisans (*maestranze*) under a goldsmith named d'Alessi gained control of the city, but dissensions brought about his death and the collapse of the insurrection. In 1674 the long-standing rivalry between the administrative capital, Palermo, and the rich silk-producing city of Messina (virtually an independent state under a close oligarchy of merchant aristocrats) came to open warfare, in which the Messinese were worsted.

In the kingdom of Naples, parliament, which had the same tripartite form as in Sicily, was no longer convoked after 1642, the function of voting taxes falling to ancient civic institutions known as the *seggi* ('sessions' or 'boards'), which were six in number, five for the city and rural nobility, and one, *il popolo*, for the richer middle class. Power was kept effectively in the hands of the viceroy by fostering class and factional divisions, which were endemic in the kingdom. Yet even a great viceroy like Pedro di Toledo, a benefactor to Naples, was unable to withstand the unanimity of popular feeling aroused against the Spanish Inquisition. As in other parts of Spanish Italy, support was gained by the bestowal of grandiose titles and lucrative public offices. High taxation, heavy duties, export restrictions and currency depreciation ruined the economy; nor was the exchequer the chief beneficiary of the large sums raised in taxation, since most of the proceeds went to the tax-farmers and government creditors, principally Genoese. Again, taxes fell heavily on the poorest classes, the nobility and the Church being virtually exempt, and insurrections in 1647–48, particularly that led by a young

146

The revolution in Naples against the Spaniards, led by the ▶
Amalfitan fisherman, Masaniello, in July 1647.

fisherman, Masaniello, were only put down with difficulty. Famine was followed by epidemics of plague, one of the worst outbreaks being in 1656, when some 300,000 were reported to have died.

A marked Spanish influence prevailed, not only on Neapolitan manners and customs, but also on art and literature. In painting, the violent, dramatic, realistic and tenebrist qualities of Caravaggio (1573–1610) found a sympathetic response in Caracciolo (d. 1637), the Spaniard Ribera (d. 1652), Mattia Preti (d. 1699), and in the sombre, romantic landscapes and macabre allegories of Salvator Rosa (d. 1673). In poetry the taste for far-fetched artifice, hyperbole and extravagant conceits was indulged by G. B. Marino (d. 1625; *L'Adone*) and his seventeenth-century followers.

By the general consent of contemporaries the ecclesiastical government of the Papal States was the worst in Italy. This was the age of the great nepotist Popes, when the papal power was at the disposal of cardinal nephews, who amassed princely fortunes at the expense of the Church – Aldobrandini, Borghese, Ludovisio, Barberini, Pamfili, Chigi: the gains of these families were more lasting than those of the Borgia or Medici. The Spanish influence, Jesuit education, the Inquisition and the *Index* stifled much originality of speculative thought. Of the three southern Italian philosophers, Telesio (d. 1588) had his books placed on the *Index*, Giordano Bruno (d. 1600) was burnt at the stake, and Tommaso Campanella (d. 1639), the author of the utopian *Città del Sole*, spent thirty years in prison for alleged conspiracy against Spain.

In 1597 the ancient d'Este duchy of Ferrara, in default of heirs in the direct line, lapsed to the Church, the duke's cousin retiring to the imperial fief of Modena; a similar fate befell the della Rovere dukes of Urbino in 1624. The ruinous financial system of the papacy reached at the end of the seventeenth century the absurd position in which interest on the public loans (*monti*) absorbed five-eighths of the annual revenue. The reforms brought about by Pope Innocent XII (Pignatelli, 1691–1700), while they stopped the worst abuses of nepotism, were unable to instil vigour into a stagnant society.

The form of the restored Medicean régime in Tuscany was firmly drawn by Duke Cosimo I (1537–74). The Tuscan state was a centralized paternal autocracy, with the court modelled on the stiff ceremonial and etiquette of the Spanish type. Cosimo permitted no political parties and his spies were everywhere. Nevertheless, except in his relations with enemies such as the Strozzi, who were exiled or put to death, his rule was impartial, and the subject towns were treated on an equality with Florence. Harbours were constructed at Porto Ferraio on Elba and at Leghorn; and works of drainage and land reclamation in the Maremma and Val di Chiana helped agriculture. Siena, which had revolted against its Spanish garrison, was taken and granted to Cosimo as an imperial fief; and his augmented status was recognized by Pope Pius V with the title of grand duke of Tuscany (1569). In the tradition of their house, the Medici grand dukes were patrons of art, letters and science. Great interest in scientific experiments was shown by Francesco (d. 1587), Cosimo II (d. 1621), who befriended Galileo, Ferdinand II (d. 1670) and his brother Leopold. The last two founded the scientific Accademia del Cimento (1657), whose published proceedings record discoveries made in pursuance of Galileo's experimental methods.

The triumphal entry of Cosimo I de' Medici, Duke of Tuscany, ▶
into Siena on 19 July 1557.

The Spanish Inquisition during the sixteenth century. From a Dutch engraving.

Venice and Genoa With the establishment of Spanish supremacy in the peninsula, the republic of Venice, whose mainland possessions adjoined those of the Habsburgs to the north and west, followed a policy of extreme caution in Italy and reserved her strength in order to maintain her eastern trading interests against the Turks. To meet the hostility of Spain and Austria, Venetian diplomacy was directed to an understanding with France. The precariousness of her political position was the ground for a stringent revision of her oligarchic institutions. The earlier councils were retained – the grand council, the senate and the *signoria* (the last consisting of the doge, three criminal judges and six ducal councillors). To the notorious Council of Ten were later added (1539) three inquisitors of state. A further organ to assist the Senate was the *collegio*, set up in about 1440, with its three committees for foreign affairs, the marine, and internal matters; the *collegio*, with the *signoria*, together known as the 'full *collegio*', became the supreme organ of government.

The Venetians were zealous in preventing papal interference in matters of state. Although the Roman Inquisition was instituted in 1547, three 'lay

A reception in the Sala del Collegio, Ducal Palace, Venice. Seventeenth century.

Left: Andrea Doria, Genoese admiral and statesman (1468–1560). *Right:* Obverse of medal commemorating the victory of Venice and her allies over the Turks at Lepanto in 1571.

assessors' were appointed to safeguard the liberties of citizens. However, in the quarrel between Pope Paul V and the republic on matters affecting the temporal jurisdiction of the state, the widely read writings of the learned Servite Paolo Sarpi (1552–1623) successfully defended the actions of the Venetians.

Although Venice and her allies achieved a victory at Lepanto (7 October 1571), the check to the Turkish advance was only temporary. During the stubborn and prolonged defence of Crete (1645–69), Venice's last major overseas possession, Venetian fleets won several victories over the Turks in the Dardanelles, but their commander, Francesco Morosini, was eventually forced to surrender. Morosini had his revenge on the Turks seventeen years later, when he recaptured the Peloponnese and Attica, being rewarded with the title *Peloponnesiaco.* But by the Treaty of Passarowitz (1718), of all her maritime empire Venice retained only Corfu, Cephalonia, Zante, Istria and the Dalmatian coast. Despite not infrequent naval victories and, during intervals of peace, the resumption of her trade with the Levant, Venetian weakness was apparent; increasing numbers of her noble families, following the trend seen elsewhere in Italy, turned from trade as beneath their dignity and invested their money in banking or in mainland property.

Venice's rival, the republic of Genoa, became the permanent ally of Spain (1528) under the leadership of Andrea Doria, who gave the state a new constitution – oligarchic, but liberalized by the possibility of creating new noble families – which with few modifications survived until the French Revolution, and which showed itself strong enough to resist the French and Savoyards and such attacks as that led by the Austrian (but Genoese-born) general Botta Adorno in 1746. Although her former empire was reduced to the sole possession of Corsica, an island which, through its economic and social backwardness, was more of a liability than an asset, Genoa grew rich as Venice declined. The Genoese were tax-farmers and bankers to the Habsburgs and their leading families gained fortunes at the expense of the impoverished subjects of Spain.

Savoy-Piedmont The founder of the (probably) Teutonic house of Savoy was Umberto Biancamano (d. *c.* 1056), who, possessing fiefs on the French and Swiss side of the Alps, as well as in the Val d'Aosta, commanded the passes of Mont Cenis and the two St Bernard passes. Marriages brought the counts valuable accessions in Piedmont. As Ghibellines, supporters of the Hohenstaufen, the counts of Savoy were appointed Vicars imperial, and thus steadily built up their possessions and prestige. Amadeo VIII was created duke (1416) by the Emperor Sigismund.

Map published in France 1515, illustrating French interest in the passes by which armies might invade Italy.

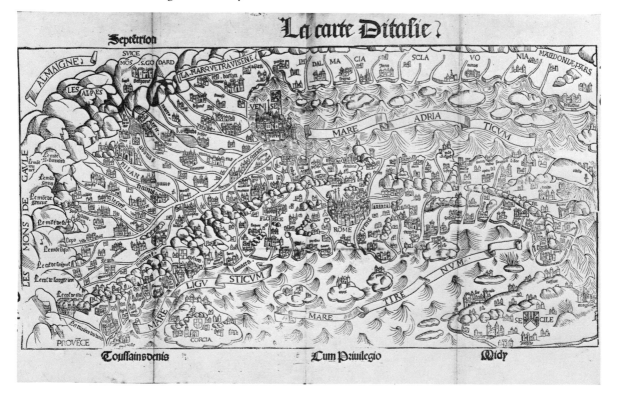

In the French invasions of Italy, the duchy of Savoy had been overrun and occupied; but Emanuel Filibert, commanding the imperial troops in the Low Countries, defeated the French at St Quentin in 1557; and at the Treaty of Cateau-Cambrésis he was rewarded by the partial restoration of his state. His son, Carlo Emanuele I, adopted the opportunist policy which became traditional in his house, of intervening in the struggles between France and the Habsburgs in Lombardy, where the support of Savoy was at times decisive. A long period of weakness under the regency (1638–55) of the French-born Duchess Christina, however, left her son, Carlo Emanuele II, powerless to save Savoy from becoming a battlefield between France and Spain.

Duke Vittorio Amadeo II of Savoy-Piedmont (1675–1732).

Louis XIV regarded Carlo Emanuele's young successor, Vittorio Amadeo II (1675–1732), as his vassal, even obliging him to persecute his Waldensian subjects. In 1690 Vittorio Amadeo felt strong enough to throw off his tutelage and to join the Grand Alliance against France. The war went unfavourably for Savoy and in 1696 the duke, accepting Louis's offer of additional territory, deserted the allies for the side of France. In the War of the Spanish Succession which followed, Savoy first supported Louis, but was detached from the French alliance by superior Austrian bribes; whereupon the French invaded Piedmont, only to be decisively defeated at Turin by Vittorio Amadeo and his second cousin, Prince Eugene of Savoy. At the Treaty of Utrecht (1714), Vittorio Amadeo's political astuteness and military successes won him Montferrat and Sicily, with the title of king. Austria received Milan, Naples and Sardinia, and in 1720 Vittorio Amadeo was obliged to yield Sicily to her in exchange for Sardinia. It was thus as kings of Sardinia that the rulers of Savoy were officially known until the unification of Italy.

At the settlement of 1720 the powers had promised the reversion of the duchies of Tuscany and Parma to Don Carlos of Bourbon, the son of Philip V of Spain by his second wife, the Italian Elisabetta Farnese. In 1731, on the death of the heirless Farnese duke of Parma, Don Carlos took possession of the duchy and was received in Florence by the last of the Medici, Gian Gastone, as heir to Tuscany. Two years later the war over the disputed succession to Poland spread to Italy: Carlo Emanuele of Sardinia drove the Austrians from Milan, and Don Carlos, at the head of a small Spanish army, expelled the Austrians from Naples and Sicily without difficulty. At the Peace of Vienna (1735) Milan was restored to Austria, the reversion to Tuscany reserved for Francis of Lorraine, the prospective husband of Maria Theresa of Austria. On the other hand, Don Carlos was confirmed in his new possession, becoming

Charles IV of Naples (1735–59). Parma and Piacenza were granted by the powers to Don Philip of Bourbon, Don Carlos's younger brother, at the Treaty of Aix-la-Chapelle (1748).

Scientific Discoveries The Italian contribution to scientific knowledge has been of the highest order. The universities of Padua (protected by Venice from the intrusion of ecclesiastics), Bologna and Pisa were of the greatest importance in the revival of scientific studies in the sixteenth and seventeenth centuries, and drew to Italy a host of foreign scholars, including, among the more famous, Copernicus, Vesalius and William Harvey. In the diffusion of scientific knowledge, printing and illustration by woodcut or engraved plates were invaluable, and woodcuts were brought to a high art in the 1543 edition of Vesalius' *Fabrica*. In mathematics the publication of the *Summa* of Luca Pacioli in 1494 began a renaissance of mathematical studies, notably after the rediscovery of the works of the Greek

Padua University. The anatomical demonstration theatre, possibly the earliest in existence (sixteenth century?). The students stood, overlooking from the tiered galleries. Corpses were brought through passages below the demonstration table.

An anatomical dissection. From a German translation of Vesalius' *Fabrica*; sixteenth century.

Archimedes (1544). The algebraical solution of equations was worked out by Scipio Ferro (d. 1526), Tartaglia (d. 1557), Cardano (whose treatise of the *Ars Magna*, 1545, is regarded as a landmark in the development of algebra) and his pupils, Ferrari and Bombelli. The mathematician G. B. della Porta (1538–1613), who is also important for his studies in optics (he has been considered the inventor of the camera obscura), founded in Naples the first scientific society, the *Accademia de' Secreti* (1560), but it fell foul of the Inquisition and was dissolved.

Galileo Galilei (1564–1642), who was appointed to the chair of mathematics at Pisa when only twenty-three, derived by means of mathematical analysis the celebrated formula, relating time, velocity and distance, in order to describe the motion of a uniformly accelerating body. Of Galileo's pupils, Torricelli (d. 1666) continued his studies in pure and applied mathematics, Viviani (d. 1703) worked on conic sections, and Borelli (d. 1679), professor of mathematics at Pisa, became widely known for his studies of animal motion, and is considered the founder of the iatro-physical school of medicine. (Torricelli

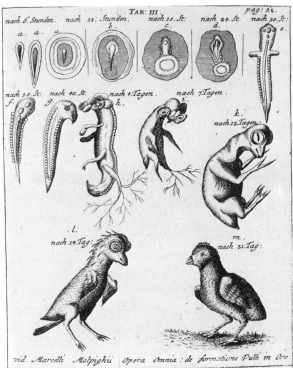

Left: Galileo Galilei. *Right:* Marcello Malpighi. Illustration of stages in the birth of a chicken. From Malpighi's *De Formatione pulli in ovo,* 1672.

invented the barometer, which Viviani constructed; and in about 1612 Galileo made his improved thermometer.) Bonaventura Cavaliere (d. 1647) of Bologna, also a pupil of Galileo, initiated steps which were completed in the infinitesimal calculus of Leibniz and Newton. In the eighteenth century Luigi Lagrange (1735–1831) of Turin won international recognition for his calculus of variations and further profound researches in pure mathematics, but his main work was done outside Italy.

In the science of optics Italy led Europe, with the work of Francisco Maurolyco of Messina (1494–1575), famous also as a mathematician, and of G. B. della Porta. The recently discovered telescope (the invention was Dutch) was employed with great effect by Galileo after 1609; and there came into use at about this time the compound microscope, with which Malpighi (d. 1694), the founder of microscopic embryology, histology, and animal and plant morphology, was able to discover the capillaries in the lungs of a frog (1661). Galileo's great work in mechanics, astronomy and in the whole field of 'natural philosophy' need only be referred to here.

In zoology Ulisse Aldrovandi of Bologna (d. 1605) was one of the leading figures of the age. Progress in botany was rapid; the first official pharmacopoeia was published in 1498 in Florence, the first botanical garden was planted in Padua (1545), and with the work of Andrea Cesalpino (1519–1603) a beginning was made in plant systemization on modern lines. Prospero Alpini (d. 1617) brought to the notice of European botanists the sexuality of plants. Following the work of Marino Ghetaldi (d. 1627), Torricelli and another of Galileo's pupils, the friar Castelli (d. 1644), made important contributions to the study of hydraulics. In all these branches of science there is seen a breaking with the Aristotelian past, a revival of direct observation and experiment, and, especially with Galileo and his school, the application of the developed mathematics to the solution of problems of physics – with revolutionary effects on traditional doctrines. The methods foreshadowed by Leonardo da Vinci were thus triumphantly vindicated.

The most advanced centre of anatomical and medical research and teaching in Europe in the sixteenth and seventeenth centuries was the University of Padua. From the time of Giovanni de Monte (1498–1552), the translator of

The water supply for the fountains of Rome. From a seventeenth-century engraving.

From *De Viribus electritatis*, 1791, by Luigi Galvani.

Galen, who gave clinical lectures on patients in the hospital of S. Francesco, a succession of great teachers occupied the chairs of anatomy and medicine, first as expositors of Galen, but then as original researchers in their own right. The greatest name was that of the Belgian-born Andrea Vesalius (1514–64), who lectured there, and also at Bologna and Pisa. Among the more distinguished of his pupils and successors were Eustachio (d. 1574), the discoverer of Eustachian tubes and valves; Columbo (d. 1560), the discoverer of the pulmonary circulation; Ingrassias (d. 1580); Aranzi (d. 1589), who has given his name to the *corpora Arantii*; Fabrizio (d. 1619), the discoverer of the valves of the veins, and the teacher of William Harvey; and Gaspar Aselli, who in 1622 first demonstrated the existence of the mesenteric veins. Malpighi, already noticed as the founder of histological anatomy, did outstanding work on the lungs, the structure of the brain, the spleen and kidney. The anatomical genius of Italy was continued in Malpighi's pupil, Valsalva, and the latter's pupil, Morgagni (d. 1771), who was famous for his great work on morbid anatomy, *De Sedibus* (1761). In Bologna the woman Laura Bassi (d. 1778) lectured on 'experimental philosophy', having as pupil her relative Lazzaro Spallanzani (d. 1799), whose experiments showed that the spermatozoa were necessary for conception and thus ended the long controversy between the 'animaculists' and the 'ovulists'. Among further valuable researches, Spallanzani demonstrated the action of gastric juices in digestion.

The terms 'galvanic', and its derivations, and 'volt' indicate the work of Italians in the science of electricity. Luigi Galvani (d. 1798) noticed the occurrence of muscular contractions in the legs of frogs in the presence of certain metals. Count Alessandro Volta (d. 1827), who was already in 1776 firing gases by electric sparks, took up Galvani's discovery and produced his 'voltaic pile', the first primary electric battery (c. 1799).

Literature and the Fine Arts

In addition to the literary and scientific societies already mentioned there were the Accademia della Crusca, founded in Florence in 1528, which devotes its activities to maintaining the purity of the Tuscan tongue, and the Accademia dei Lincei, instituted by the Marchese di Monticelli in 1603, which was originally scientific in its interests. Among the many curiously named literary societies was the Roman Accademia degli Arcadi, founded in 1690 by the Abate Crescembini and the distinguished jurist Gravina with the aim of superseding the flatulent seventeenth-century poetry by the cultivation of simplicity and a pastoral naturalness. Nothing illustrates better the artificiality

Stage décor in the eighteenth century. The opera *The Marriage of Thetis and Peleus*, given before the French royal court. Designed by Giacomo Torelli.

of the age than this conscious replacement of one kind of artifice by another. A favourite verse form was the *canzonetta*, which was used with some effect by Paolo Rolli (d. 1765), and reached a high degree of polished facility in the verse of Pietro Trapassi, called Metastasio (d. 1782). Chief among writers who met the ever-increasing demands for operatic *libretti* were Apostolo Zeno (d. 1750), who also made important contributions to the history of Italian literature, and above all Metastasio, whose art was perfectly adapted to the eighteenth-century taste for reinterpreting classical themes in terms of amorous intrigue, melting sentiment and languorous passion (*Didone abbandonata*, *Clemenza di Tito*). Outgrowing Arcadia, the priest Giuseppe Parini (d. 1799) gave hints of a new vigour in lyrical verse with his *Odi*, and produced in the controlled irony of his poem *Il Giorno* an effective satire on the inanity of the upper classes.

The full force of poetic reaction to Arcadia came with the tragic drama of Count Vittorio Alfieri (d. 1803), whose classical subjects were the occasion for attacks on political tyranny and for a call for a resurgent patriotism. With the Venetian Goldoni (d. 1793) the *commedia dell'arte* developed into a true comedy of manners (*La bottega del caffè*, *La locandiera*), pungent, earthy, mildly satirical. In fierce opposition to Goldoni's bourgeois world was his fellow Venetian, Count Carlo Gozzi (d. 1806), who, also taking the *commedia dell'arte* as his starting-point, transformed it into a fantasy of fable and satire (*L'amore delle tre melarance*, *L'augellino verde*).

159

Prison of St Michael, Rome. This prison (altered in the eighteenth century), and the writings of Giovanni Beccaria, influenced the English prison reformer John Howard.

The regno of Naples has always given Italy some of its foremost thinkers. In G. B. Vico (1668–1744), it produced a social philosopher of great originality, who in his *Scienza nuova* attempted to account historically for the essential identity but undoubted development of systems of law. He found his solution to the problem in the historical evolution of laws in correspondence with the evolution of societies, and with the evolution of man both socially and psychologically. The Neapolitan historian Giannone (d. 1748) sketched the development of Neapolitan political institutions in his *Storia del Regno di Napoli*, but his criticism of ecclesiastical policies in the kingdom led to his imprisonment. A new, positivist approach to historical studies was opened by L. A. Muratori (d. 1750), who made available to scholars his great collection of medieval texts in *Rerum Italicarum Scriptores*.

The ideas of the eighteenth-century Enlightenment were received in Italy among members of the educated classes and, although not penetrating deeply into society, had a notable effect on such writers as Antonio Genovesi (d. 1796), who held in Naples the first European professorship in economics; the Abate Galliani (d. 1787), another Neapolitan, an economist and wit; Gaetano Filangieri (d. 1788), also of Naples, whose work, *La Scienza della legislazione*, and whose own social position gave him freedom to criticize current abuses; and Giuseppe Beccaria (d. 1794), the Milanese author of a book epoch-making in its humanitarian influence on penal reform.

In the seventeenth and eighteenth centuries the development of Italian opera moved concurrently with that of purely instrumental music in the form of the sonata, the concerto, ensembles of several instruments, and the symphony. The quality of string music was greatly improved by the production of the violin-makers of Cremona: the Amati family, followed by members of the Guarneri and Stradivari families. In about 1709 the Florentine Cristofori invented the piano (*gravicembalo con piano e forte*). In opera the Italians held their own until the advent of Gluck (b. 1714); the Florentine Lulli (d. 1687) was the effective founder of French opera, as Duni (d. 1775) from Basilicata was of French *opéra bouffe*. The first outstanding composer of *opera buffa* was G. B. Pergolesi (d. 1736), whose *La Serva Padrona* was produced in Naples in 1733; its popularity led to other works in the same genre, notably *Il Barbiere di Siviglia* by Paisiello (d. 1816) and *Il Matrimonio Segreto* by Cimarosa (d. 1801). Among the great number of Italian composers of this period to win European recognition were Stradella (d. 1682), Corelli (d. 1713), Marcello (d. 1739), Vivaldi (d. 1741), Domenico Scarlatti (d. 1757), Jommelli (d. 1774), Sacchini (d. 1786) and Clementi (d. 1832).

In painting, although Italy in the seventeenth and eighteenth centuries drew scores of visiting foreign artists (including Poussin and Claude Lorrain, who might be considered Italian painters), native artists seldom rose above the mediocre. The Neapolitan Solimena (d. 1747) has his admirers; but it was in Venice that the rococo period was seen at its best in the work of Tiepolo (d. 1770). The canals and façades of Venice were the subjects for the subtle colouring and precision of detail of Antonio Canaletto (d. 1768), and, treated more in an impressionist manner, of Francesco Guardi (d. 1793). Another Venetian, the engraver Piranesi (d. 1778), who worked in Rome, produced

From the *Carceri d'Invenzione*, by the Venetian engraver Giambattista Piranesi.

architectural drawings of great dramatic and graphic power, particularly in the series of imaginary prisons, *Carceri d'invenzione*. In architecture the Dutch-Italian Vanvitelli (d. 1773) showed a feeling for the monumental in the Bourbon palace at Caserta. At this period Rome was adorned with the delightful Spanish Steps (1721) to the designs of Specchi and de Sanctis, and with the popular Fountain of Trevi, perhaps the joint work of Salvi and Fuga. Little of value was achieved in sculpture, the neo-classical work of Canova (1757–1832) belonging properly to the succeeding period.

Politics and Society in the Eighteenth Century

From 1748 – when the Treaty of Aix-la-Chapelle closed the War of the Austrian Succession, and Maria Theresa was securely established on her throne – until the coming of Bonaparte in 1796, Italy enjoyed a respite from foreign wars fought on her soil. During this period, under the influence of the general European movement of the Enlightenment, the Italian dynastic rulers, while occupied with increasing their absolutism by strong centralized governments, none the less sought to win the support of public opinion by a measure of reform. The ecclesiastical power was seen as the main obstacle to progress: Jansenist infiltration, the founding of Freemason lodges and a resuscitation of the Conciliar movement weakened the Church, which, on the expulsion of the Jesuits from Portugal and the Bourbon states, was forced to dissolve the Society of Jesus in 1773. The republics of Venice and Genoa, the kingdom of Sardinia and the possessions of the Estensi were in general outside the movement towards reform. In Savoy and Sardinia the government of Vittorio Amadeo II and of his son Carlo Emanuele III had carried through reforms in the economic, legal, educational and ecclesiastical fields, but under Vittorio Amadeo III (1773–96) a narrow autocracy and militarism prevailed. Genoa, suffering from an economic and political decline, was compelled to seek French aid to repress revolts in Corsica (1735–69), and ultimately, after the exile of the rebel leader, Pasquale Paoli, to cede the sovereignty of the island to the French (May 1768). Nowhere was the falling-off in economic and civic affairs so marked as in Venice, where the splendid monuments of its former greatness served but as a backcloth to what was becoming the bagnio of an effete aristocracy and of leisured foreigners. Italy remained, more than ever, the goal of the grand tour, and a knowledge of the country was indispensable for the completion of an aristocratic education. Those Italians who gained an international reputation were more often than not musicians, or adventurers like Cagliostro and Casanova.

King Ferdinand I of the Two Sicilies (Ferdinand IV of Naples), with Queen Maria
Carolina and their children. By Angelica Kauffmann (1741–1807).

Notwithstanding these signs of inertia, or on occasion of positive reaction, it
is undeniable that progress was made in those states subject to the houses of
Habsburg-Lorraine (Milan, Tuscany, Modena) and of Bourbon (Naples,
Sicily, Parma). In Milan the government of Count Firmian introduced a
series of bold measures: the administration was remodelled, a census was
taken, taxation was more justly distributed, agriculture and industry were
encouraged, the Inquisition was abolished and ecclesiastical abuses were
curtailed. Economic life quickly revived in Lombardy. A similar amelioration
in the condition of Tuscany occurred under the reforming, but strictly paternal-
ist, government set up by Francis of Lorraine, and of his son Peter Leopold.
Tuscany was the first European state to adopt the humanitarian ideas of Beccaria, abolishing the death penalty and the use of torture. No class of citizens
was exempt from taxation and accounts were published of public receipts and
expenditure.

The rule of Don Philip, the first Bourbon duke of Parma, was likewise
beneficent under the Frenchman Du Tillot, but this minister was forced to
resign (1771) on the accession of Don Philip's son Don Ferdinand, married to
Maria Theresa's daughter, Maria Amelia. To Naples and Sicily Charles IV

The royal palace at Caserta. Fountain, 'The Diana Group', by several sculptors.

brought with him as his chief minister an able, anti-clerical Tuscan, Bernardo Tanucci, who attempted to produce some order out of the chaos of privileges, exemptions, immunities and legal anomalies that were the heritage of centuries of dynastic changes. In this he was only partially successful, since he was opposed by the nobility, the Church, the numerous lawyer class, the superstitious plebeians, and – after Charles's accession to the Spanish throne and the minority of his son Ferdinand IV – by the latter's wife Maria Carolina, another of Maria Theresa's daughters. It was Maria Carolina, who, profiting by the indolence of Ferdinand, engineered Tanucci's resignation (1776) and the appointment as chief minister of the Englishman Sir John Acton. The reign of Charles IV brought a resurgence in economic life, mainly in that of Naples. Charles was an indefatigable builder (as can be seen in the Palaces of Caserta and Capodimonte, the Albergo dei Poveri and Teatro S. Carlo), and the presence of a royal court did much to revive the social and intellectual life of the

Eighteenth-century engraving showing the excavation of the Temple of Isis at Pompeii.

capital. The excavation of Pompeii and Herculaneum brought to light splendid works of classical art, which went to augment the Farnese collections which Charles had inherited. Naples became an international metropolis, the residence of many rich and aristocratic foreigners.

In Sicily, under the enlightened viceroy, Caracciolo, attempts were made at administrative and ecclesiastical reform, but the entrenched opposition of nobles and ecclesiastics limited any radical change. With Ferdinand and Maria Carolina – particularly the latter, whose imperious will dominated the easy-going king – Naples moved away from the Spanish orientation of its foreign policy in the direction of Austria. More liberal tendencies among the upper classes became increasingly suspect; and the outbreak of the French Revolution in 1789 and the execution of the French royal couple in 1793 (Marie Antoinette was Maria Carolina's sister) were followed by a further tightening of internal reaction.

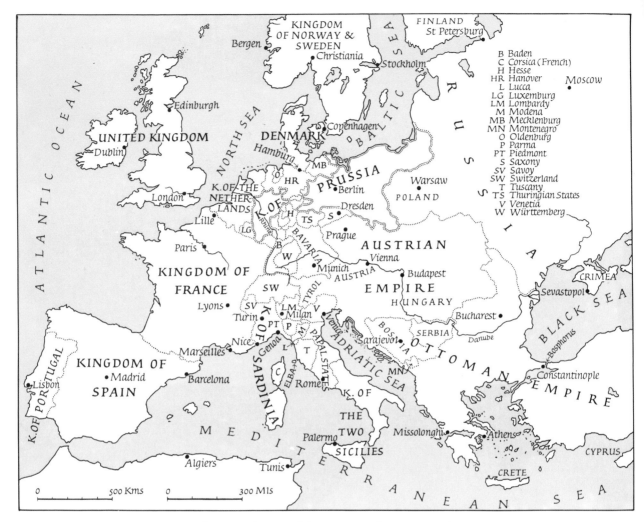

Europe after the settlement of the Congress of Vienna (1815).

Chapter Seven

RESURGENCE AND RETRIBUTION, 1796–1948

In the spring of 1796 the Corsican-born Napoleon Bonaparte (spelled Buona-parte until that year), at the head of the army of revolutionary France, invaded Piedmont and Austrian Lombardy, and with astounding rapidity made him-self master of northern Italy. Risings among upper- and middle-class 'Jacobin' sympathizers in Modena, Reggio, Ferrara and Bologna led to the founding of the so-called Cispadane republic, which Napoleon amalgamated with his Transpadane republic (created from the territories of Milan, Mantua, Bergamo, Brescia and Crema) to form the Cisalpine republic. Yielding to French menaces, the ancient republic of Venice voted for its own extinction and its territory was transferred by Napoleon to Austria by the Treaty of Campo For-mio (October 1797). In February 1798 Pope Pius VI was driven into exile and a Roman republic proclaimed under French auspices. Ferdinand IV of Naples, stirred into action by his queen, attacked the French commanded by Champion-net, but was soon in headlong flight, from which he did not pause until he was safe in Sicily under English protection. Despite a heroic resistance by the *lazzaroni*, Championnet entered Naples and, finding support among the educated classes, established the short-lived Parthenopean republic. The successes of the army of the Second Coalition, under the Russian veteran Suvarov, against the French in Lombardy in the spring of 1799, and the advance from Calabria of Cardinal Ruffo and his Sanfedisti, brought about its collapse (June), an event followed by bloody reprisals. By the end of the year only Genoa remained in French hands, and Italian liberals were left at the mercy of restored Habsburgs and Bourbons.

Bonaparte, back in France from Egypt, had succeeded in making himself head of the state by the *coup d'état* of Brumaire (10 November 1799). As First

Pope Pius VI ordered into exile by the Directorate, 13 February 1798.

Consul, he returned to Lombardy in May 1800 and in the following month won the resounding victory of Marengo. The political reshaping of the Italian states was achieved at his dictation; but it was not until he had crowned himself emperor of the French (December 1804) and defeated the Third Coalition on the field of Austerlitz (December 1805) that his reconstruction of Italy was effected. The kingdom of Naples was given to the emperor's brother Joseph, the Bourbons again having retired to Sicily. On Joseph's departure for the throne of Spain in 1808, he was succeeded by Murat. Piedmont, Liguria, Parma, Tuscany, Umbria and Lazio (with Rome) were annexed directly to France. The kingdom of Italy, under Eugène Beauharnais as Napoleon's viceroy, included Lombardy, Venice, the former Papal Legations (Bologna, Ferrara, Ravenna and Forlì) and an eastern coastal strip as far south as the River Tronto. Protected by the British fleet, Sardinia remained with the house of Savoy (whose ruler was Vittorio Emanuele I) and Sicily with the Bourbons of Naples.

Napoleon Bonaparte as
First Consul, 1803.

Napoleon crowning himself King of Italy in Milan, 26 May 1805.

The ex-Empress Marie Louise, Duchess of Parma. Daguerrotype taken in Rome by the first Italian photographer in 1847, three months before her death.

The Congress of Vienna, which followed the collapse of Napoleonic power in 1814–15, proceeded to settle the affairs of Europe on the basis of dynastic sovereignty and the balance of power. In Italy Vittorio Emanuele I received, in addition to his hereditary states, Genoa, Nice and the Ligurian littoral. The 'Kingdom of Lombardy-Venetia' was formed into provinces of the Habsburg empire. Naples and Sicily were restored to the Bourbons, the king (Ferdinand IV) adopting the new style of Ferdinand I of the Two Sicilies. The princes of

The French in Venice, 1806. The bronze horses are being removed from St Mark's.

Habsburg-Lorraine returned to their states: Ferdinand III to the grand duchy of Tuscany, Francis IV to the duchy of Modena. Parma was created a duchy for Marie Louise, the wife of the fallen Napoleon; the little duchy of Lucca was given to Marie Louise of Bourbon. Finally, Pope Pius VII regained Rome and the Papal States.

Politically this settlement appeared to be a restoration of the *status quo ante*, but in reality the period of French domination had effects of a far-reaching political and social nature. Napoleon had fractured the old state system with its provincial exclusiveness, creating uniformities in the law (the abolition of feudalism, the establishment of civil equality and the Code Napoléon), in economic life (the removal of customs barriers, the introduction of the metric system, the encouragement of capitalism), in bureaucratic administration, in the armed forces, in the building of roads, bridges, canals and monuments. All these innovations had a positive effect towards promoting a national sentiment. Nor did the negative side of French rule fail to arouse something of a feeling of *italianità*: consciousness of political impotence was widespread among the educated classes; conscription in the Napoleonic armies (by 1812 91,000 Italians had been recruited), especially after the Peninsular and Russian campaigns, where Italian losses were 22,000 and 26,000 respectively, brought a realization of national identity both in action and in bereavement; people felt strongly about high taxation, the removal of art treasures to France, and even the humiliations suffered by Italian Popes. All these different factors served to offset

The return of Pope Pius VII to Rome on 24 May 1814, after Napoleon's fall.

Left: Giuseppe Mazzini, the founder of the 'Association of Young Italy'. A curious 'psychographic portrait'.

Right: A meeting of a lodge of the Carbonari, *c.* 1820. The initiates are seated on the left, the 'masters' (*capi*) on the right.

the gains from French rule and to produce a common resentment (however inarticulate or ineffectual) that for one man's ambition *Italian* interests had been sacrificed.

This discontent resulted in the formation of secret political societies, favouring constitutional government and independence from foreign rule: the Carbonari in the south found support in other parts of Italy, becoming affiliated with such groups as the Guelfi, Adelfi or the Federati, and inspired the revolts which took place in Italy between 1820 and 1832. Insurrections in Naples and Turin in 1820, where demands were raised for a constitution based on the recently granted Spanish model, were suppressed by Austrian arms; this was in accordance with Metternich's policy of intervention to maintain dynastic authority against dangers of contagious 'liberalism'. Again, in 1831 Austrian forces quelled revolutions which spread from Modena to the Papal Legations.

The vagueness of aim and weakness in organization of the Carbonari were demonstrated by these failures, so that many of the more ardent revolutionaries turned to the doctrines propounded by the Genoese political exile Giuseppe Mazzini (1802–72), the founder of the Association of Young Italy (La Giovane Italia), whose declared aim was to constitute 'Italy one free, independent, republican nation'. An early convert to the movement was the Niçois Giuseppe

172

Garibaldi (1807–82). Mazzini promoted insurrections in Piedmont (1833, 1834), the Two Sicilies (1837, 1841, 1844, 1857) and the Papal States (1843, 1845). Although the sacrifices of Mazzinian idealists such as the Bandiera brothers and Carlo Pisacane brought Italian affairs to the notice of Europe, the movement lacked wide support in the country and was opposed by many as being too revolutionary and doctrinaire.

More moderate counsels for the solution of Italy's problems were those of the federalist 'neo-Guelf' Vincenzo Gioberti, who wrote on the 'moral and civil primacy of the Italians'; of Count Cesare Balbo, expressed in his book, *Delle speranze d'Italia*; of the empirical thinkers Carlo Cattaneo, Giuseppe Ferrari and Count Carlo Pettiti; and of the novelist, painter and later prime minister, Massimo d'Azeglio. Others who advanced the cause of Italian unity were the poets Ugo Foscolo, Giuseppe Giusti and Giovanni Berchet, and the writers Silvio Pellico, who described his term of imprisonment in the Spielberg in *Le mie prigioni* (1832), and Alessandro Manzoni, whose famous novel *I promessi sposi*, written first in Milanese but later revised in Tuscan, did as much to foster a national feeling as it did to develop a common Italian language. In a class apart was the profound poetry of Giacomo Leopardi (1798–1837), one of the greatest of Italian poets.

The revolution of 1848 in Naples, just before the attack of 15 May.

The accession in 1846 of the 'liberal' Giovanni Mastai-Ferretti as Pope Pius IX (Pio Nono) was the occasion for an amnesty of political prisoners and a granting of a measure of freedom of the press; there seemed even a prospect of constitutional government. A rising in Palermo in January 1848, when shouts were raised of 'Long live Italy, the Sicilian constitution and Pio Nono!', was followed by successful revolts elsewhere in Sicily and in a matter of days practically the whole island was in revolutionary hands. Further agitation in Naples forced Ferdinand II to grant a constitution to the Two Sicilies and the king in person swore to maintain it (10 February 1848). The Paris revolution in the same month was the signal for uprisings throughout Europe. Carlo Alberto of Savoy promulgated a constitution (the 'Albertine *Statuto*') on 4 March. The grand duke of Tuscany and the Pope were constrained to follow suit. On 13 March news reached Italy of a revolution in Vienna and the flight of Metternich. Four days later Venice was proclaimed a republic under Daniele Manin and Nicolò Tommaseo; and in the heroic 'Five Days' (18–22 March) the people of Milan rose and drove out the Austrians.

The bombardment of Venice by the Austrians, 1849. A republic had been proclaimed under Manin and Tommaseo.

When on 23 March Carlo Alberto declared war on Austria for the liberation of Italy, the forces of Piedmont-Sardinia were joined by volunteers from all regions, including at first Naples and the Papal States. In an allocution of 29 April, however, the Pope declared his neutrality, and Ferdinand of Naples took the occasion to order the withdrawal of his troops. The war revealed, besides military incompetence in the higher command, a conflict of interest between revolutionary republicans and monarchists, and a lack of confidence in Piedmont's liberating role. A minor military reverse at Custozza turned into a demoralized withdrawal and defeat. An armistice was signed at Salasco and Lombardy was once more subject to Austrian rule; Venice, however, continued to hold out until August 1849.

In Naples Ferdinand seized an opportunity offered him by an attempted revolt to dissolve parliament and abrogate the constitution; and in September 1848 the Sicilian insurgents were repressed with such vigour as to earn him the title 'King Bomba'. Later in the same year the Pope fled to Gaeta in Neapolitan territory, where he was joined in exile by the grand duke of Tuscany. In Rome a republic was established, with Mazzini, who had been made an honorary citizen, as one of the guiding triumvirs. On the cessation of fighting in Lombardy, Garibaldi led a contingent of volunteers to the defence of the Roman republic, which was threatened by the intervention of French troops sent by Louis Napoleon. Although he was defeated by the numerical superiority of the besieging forces, Garibaldi's defence of Rome and his subsequent escape did much to raise Italian morale. Carlo Alberto, pressed by the parliamentary left and personally determined to wipe out the shame of defeat, suddenly denounced the Salasco armistice on 12 March 1849. Yet once again the main result was to demonstrate the inefficiency of the Piedmontese army. At Novara, Carlo Alberto was decisively beaten and immediately abdicated in favour of his son Vittorio Emanuele II.

By the end of 1849 the Piedmontese parliament was the only constitutional body remaining in the country. It was to become the instrument through which the unification of Italy was achieved at the hands of a consummate master of political and diplomatic finesse. Count Camillo Benso di Cavour (1810–61) was educated for the army, but he resigned his commission at twenty-one and travelled in England, France and Belgium, before settling down to manage his brother's estate at Leri and to interest himself in banking and industry. During the reign of Carlo Alberto, who disliked Cavour's liberalism, he avoided politics, but was already influential in the country through two of his foundations, the Piedmontese Agricultural Society and the newspaper *Il Risorgimento* (Resurgence).

He entered parliament in 1848 and accepted cabinet rank two years later as minister of agriculture and industry under Massimo d'Azeglio. The long-term intention of the two statesmen was to show Italy and the world that Piedmont-Sardinia, although a monarchy, was a stable, progressive and modern state, and one capable of leading the country to unity. Cavour, finding d'Azeglio too conservative and cautious, moved towards the left-centre led by Urbano Rattazzi, this 'marriage' (*connubio*) of liberal-conservatives provoking a split with d'Azeglio and the right. Cavour succeeded d'Azeglio as prime minister in 1852. The avowed policy of the Cavour-Rattazzi coalition was to 'prepare the way for Piedmont to liberate Italy from foreign rule'. Cavour, who possessed, in addition to a detailed grasp of the realities of international affairs, an uncanny intuition of how any diplomatic negotiation could be made to yield the greatest political advantage, proceeded patiently to lay the mine which would cause the required explosion – the simile is his. His diplomatic method was so to place

Left: Count Camillo Benso Cavour. *Right:* The first issue of Cavour's newspaper,
Il Risorgimento. The leading article was written by Cesare Balbo.

himself that the resolution of a critical situation would find him in the position
of the *tertius gaudens*.

Unable alone to defeat Austria, Piedmont had to secure allies. When in
1855 Cavour, against powerful opposition, sent Piedmontese soldiers to fight
beside the French and British in the Crimean War, his motive was partly to
ensure a seat among the powers at the prospective peace conference, although
more immediately to prevent the king from dismissing him. At the Congress of
Paris he brought the Italian question before the conference and sounded the
possibility of English and French support against Austria. In 1857 Giuseppe
La Farina founded the National Society, which brought together even republicans like Manin, Pallavicino and Garibaldi (but not Mazzini) in favour of a
Piedmont-inspired policy. Cavour worked with great skill in cultivating the
friendship of Louis Napoleon, especially when intense diplomatic pressure
was put on Piedmont to curb the liberty of its press at the time of Felice Orsini's
attempt on the life of Napoleon (January 1858). A secret meeting between the

177

The attempt on the life of the Emperor Napoleon III by Felice Orsini, 14 January 1858.

emperor and Cavour took place in July 1859 at Plombières, a resort in the Vosges; there it was agreed that the French would aid Piedmont against Austria ('to free Italy from the Alps to the Adriatic'), if it could be represented to the world that Austria was the aggressor. The Piedmontese army was quietly mobilized and Garibaldi, gazetted as a major-general, was given command of a volunteer corps (Cacciatori delle Alpi). The Austrians looked on this recruiting and arming of volunteers as a direct provocation, as Cavour had intended they should view it. At this juncture the proposal of the powers that a congress should be called to maintain peace seemed to put Cavour's plans in jeopardy; but his adroitness enabled him to overcome this diplomatic move.

Finally Austria placed herself in the wrong in the world's opinion, when a unilateral demand for Piedmont to disarm was sent as an ultimatum. Cavour was thus in the position to call on Napoleon to fulfil his pledge (27 April 1859). The day after the outbreak of hostilities the Florentines, under the leadership of Baron Ricasoli, expelled the grand duke, and Piedmont assumed a

Italy in 1870, showing the dates of annexation of the states.

The battle of Solferino. Painting by C. Bossoli, 1859.

protectorate over Tuscany. Following the allied victory of Magenta in June, Parma and Modena rose against their princes and asked for union with Piedmont; Romagna likewise overthrew the papal government and joined the movement for north Italian unity. These actions were the result of careful preparatory work by the National Society, acting in close concert with Cavour. After another allied victory at Solferino, Napoleon, fearing to commit himself further, concluded an armistice with the Austrian emperor at Villafranca (11 July 1859). Negotiations between the French and Austrians had been conducted independently of King Vittorio Emanuele; and on receipt of the news Cavour, after an angry scene with the king, resigned.

In spite of the armistice terms, whereby only Lombardy (with the exception of Mantua and Peschiera) was to go to Piedmont, the insurgent states maintained their provisional governments and by plebiscites voted for annexation to Piedmont. Louis Napoleon was only brought round to accept this enlarged kingdom at the price of the cession of Savoy and Nice to France. Cavour, who returned

The embarkation of Garibaldi's 'Thousand' near Genoa, 5 May 1860. Painting by G. Induno.

to office in January 1860, reluctantly agreed and carried the unpopular measure
through parliament. The actions of Garibaldi and his 'Thousand' were neither
controlled nor openly favoured by Cavour; he could only look on and await
events. The temerity of Garibaldi's expedition in support of the rebelling
Sicilians, with a handful of ill-equipped volunteers against 25,000 regular
Bourbon troops, was matched by its outstanding success. Landing at Marsala,
he defeated the Bourbon forces in a hard-fought engagement at Calatafimi on
15 May, and the way was open to Palermo, which fell twelve days later. Garibaldi assumed a dictatorship in the name of 'Italy and Vittorio Emanuele',
and Cavour's attempts to interfere in the island were rudely repulsed.

In late August Garibaldi crossed from Sicily into Calabria, where risings
in the province, and also in Apulia, aided him in his rapid march on Naples,
which he entered on 7 September, King Francesco II and his queen having the
previous day left to join the Bourbon army on the River Volturno. Cavour,
determined to forestall any Garibaldian attack on Rome, used the presence there

Right: Giuseppe Garibaldi.
Engraving by W. Holl,
after a photograph, 1856.

Below: The triumphal entry of
King Vittorio Emmanuele II
with 'General' Garibaldi into
Naples, 7 November 1860.

of foreign volunteers under General Lamoricière as the pretext for the Piedmontese army to invade papal Umbria (11 September). After the defeat of the papal forces at Castelfidardo and the capture of Ancona, Vittorio Emanuele crossed into Neapolitan territory (15 October) where Garibaldi had a fortnight earlier defeated the Bourbon army on the Volturno. The king and Garibaldi met outside Teano and together entered Naples (7 November); thereupon, refusing any reward, Garibaldi retired to his island of Caprera. Plebiscites in the Two Sicilies and in Umbria and the Marches overwhelmingly called for amalgamation with Piedmont; and in February 1861 the parliamentary representatives of a nation of twenty-one millions met in Turin.

Unity of the greater part of Italy had been achieved, but divisions and dissensions soon showed themselves. Chief among these were the strained relations of the new state with the papacy (the first united parliament having affirmed that Rome was ultimately to be the capital), the hostility of Mazzini and republicans to

The opening of the first Italian parliament in Turin, February 1861. After a contemporary engraving.

Piedmontese monarchical institutions, and regional differences and jealousies, particularly those arising from the disparity between social and economic conditions in northern and southern Italy. The question of regional autonomy was raised from the outset, but it was shelved in favour of the centralized system resulting from the actual annexation of the various states by Piedmont. To add to the difficulties of the new nation, there was a lack of experienced men of affairs, and Cavour's early and sudden death on 6 June 1861 left a gap that could not be filled. The new prime minister was the Tuscan Baron Ricasoli. Venetia and Rome had still to be liberated; but when in August 1862 Garibaldi tried to cut the diplomatic knot by leading a body of volunteers ('Rome or Death') from Sicily, the king, fearing international intervention, sent a force which wounded and captured him on Aspromonte in Calabria.

Faced with the formidable problem of brigandage in the south, to say nothing of difficulties inherent in the centralized state, the Italian government sought to mould public opinion by an aggressive foreign policy. In April 1866 an alliance was entered into with Prussia against Austria, and, although the latter was willing to cede Venetia as the price of neutrality, Italy forced the outbreak of a war which resulted in an Italian army of 260,000 men being defeated at Custozza by an Austrian force of half its size. Next month the incapacity of the Italian navy was shown in an engagement with an Austrian fleet of vastly inferior strength off the island of Lissa. It was the Prussian victory at Sadowa that allowed Italy to

Left: The death of Cavour on 6 June 1861 left the country leaderless. A contemporary cartoon shows prominent Italians 'in the darkness . . . with little hope of seeing the light'.

Right: Pope Pius IX ('Pio Nono', Giovanni Mastai-Ferretti, Pope, 1846–78). From a photograph.

acquire Venetia (through Napoleon III as intermediary), the territory in the Tyrol conquered by Garibaldi's contingent remaining Austrian.

At this moment a serious revolt broke out in Palermo, which required an expeditionary force to quell. Whether or not the Church was implicated in the Sicilian uprising, relations between the papacy and the Italian state, which was not recognized by the Pope, had been embittered by the encyclical *Quanta cura* and the attached Syllabus of Errors (1864), which condemned, among other things, freedom of discussion and of conscience, progress, liberalism and modern civilization. In November 1867 Garibaldi attempted to invade papal territory. To protect Rome, Napoleon ordered the return of the French forces withdrawn in 1866; and these troops, armed with the new *chassepot* rifles, defeated the Garibaldians at Mentana with a loss of only 150 men. It was the outbreak of the Franco-Prussian war in July 1870 that brought about the final withdrawal of French troops. After the Pope's refusal of a last appeal from the king, the city was entered by Italian troops on 20 September. Pio Nono shut himself in his palace, the 'prisoner of the Vatican', a plebiscite favoured the inclusion of Rome in the Italian state and in July 1871 the capital was transferred thence from Florence, where it had moved from Turin in 1864.

The constitutional monarchy set up by the Albertine *Statuto*, and after 1860 applied to the annexed regions, consisted of a senate nominated by the king and a chamber of deputies elected by a restricted franchise of some half a million, of whom only 300,000 voted – loyal Catholics, in obedience to the Pope's *Non expedit*, refraining from political life. It was perhaps inevitable that, in order to achieve and to defend the dual objectives of independence and unity, a strongly centralized state should have been set up. Like France, the country was divided into provinces under prefects, districts (*circondari*) under sub-prefects and communes headed by syndics, all these offices being at first appointments of the minister of the interior, a circumstance which led to widespread political jobbery. The high hopes which prevailed at the time of unification were quickly dissipated, as the problems of creating the administrative apparatus of a unitary state presented themselves.

The *risorgimento* had been brought about by comparatively few dedicated Italians and chiefly by the aid of foreign arms. Many Italians were apathetic, if not actively hostile, to the new state. Regional and personal interests could not be speedily and easily subordinated to national interests – particularly when a national consciousness barely existed. The unification had been costly – in money, if not in lives: the public debt in 1861 stood at 2,450 million lire; four years later it had doubled. The setting up of an administrative system, the construction of roads and railways, the war in the south against brigandage (involving the presence of 120,000 troops in 1865), and the Austrian war caused heavy deficits, which rapid increases in taxation could not bridge. In 1869 a flour tax was introduced, which fell heavily on the poorest classes, and the rioting that followed caused 250 deaths. Ecclesiastical property was confiscated and sold by the state, but this capital gain was soon exhausted. Deputies, who were unpaid, were predominantly middle class. Moreover since party lines did not correspond with social realities, the tendency was for cabinets to be formed around personalities, and, after the defeat or resignation of a prime minister, to be reshuffled in much the same mixture as before.

For the first sixteen years after 1860 the government was to the right of centre and saw its main tasks as strengthening the army (to 350,000 men) and the navy, opposing papal claims ('the Roman question'), building up industry and agriculture and, above all, balancing the budget. This last object was achieved by Minghetti in 1876, on the eve of his ministry's falling and being replaced by Depretis's first cabinet of the left. Under Depretis, who led the government (with two breaks) until 1887, was evolved a transformation (*trasformismo*) of the old party labels and a system of flagrant rigging of elections. Prefects and governmental officials, particularly in the south, were moved or threatened with removal, promises were given for preferential treatment in the awarding of state

The result of the successful *risorgimento*
and the unification of Italy: a vast
increase in taxation, mostly indirect,
as this cartoon indicates.

contracts, in providing roads, railways and schools, in order that *ministeriali* should be returned to parliament. Politics became the pursuit of the perquisites of power, deputies being representatives of sectional (often financial) interests, with the result that there was a decline in respect for parliamentary institutions. In 1877 an act was passed providing for compulsory education for children up to the age of nine, but in the south, where illiteracy was widespread, its provisions were quietly ignored. The electorate was enlarged in 1882 to something under three millions. Universal adult male suffrage was not achieved until 1912.

In foreign affairs few Italians after Cavour were realistic in assessing Italy's position in the world, although Rattazzi before his death in 1873 admitted that no one in Europe regarded Italy as a great power. Military defeats had made Italians both sensitive and aggressive. Austria, the traditional enemy, still held territories claimed by Italy (*Italia irredenta*), in particular Trentino and Trieste. Later the Istrian peninsula and Fiume – even Dalmatia – were to be claimed. In the seventies and eighties fears of French assistance in restoring the temporal power of the papacy hardened into an anti-French policy, especially when France forestalled Italy in occupying Tunis (1881), where Italians had large business interests.

Left: Agostino Depretis (1813–87), who formed the first cabinet of the left in 1876.
Right: Francesco Crispi (1819-1901), who suceeded Depretis as Prime Minister in 1887.

The principal advocate of the new alignment in Italian foreign policy was the unstable Crispi. In 1882 Depretis's government brought Italy as a very junior partner into the Triple Alliance with Austria and Germany, seeing this as an assurance against possible French aggression. Crispi indulged in what Pasquale Villari held to be some of the more dangerous of Italian political vices: rhetoric combined with megalomania, which blinded others besides himself. Succeeding Depretis as prime minister in 1887, he was responsible for beginning a tariff war with France, which did great damage to the economy of southern Italy. Fascinated by Bismarck, he paid several visits to Germany. As foreign as well as prime minister, he aimed at enhancing Italy's prestige; he wanted to give the new nation 'not only power but the reputation and consequences of power'. He gave it none of these. Mussolini was later to see in this demagogue 'the forerunner of resurgent fascist Italy'. In 1882 the Italian government took over the private commercial station of Assab on the Red Sea and in 1885 occupied the garrison of Massawa, evacuated by Egypt. Pushing inland, the Italians alarmed the negus of Ethiopia, and a border incident in 1887 led to the loss of five hundred men, surprised by Ras Alula at Dogali. Crispi, resolved on revenge, claimed an Italian protectorate over Ethiopia and actively interfered in its internal affairs. In 1889 Italy acquired a protectorate over part of Somaliland to the south of Ethiopia.

The outcome of Crispi's aggressive policy, backed by no adequate planning, was the defeat of General Baratieri at Adowa, with the loss of six thousand Italian lives (1 March 1896). On 5 March 1896 Crispi's resignation was, to his surprise, accepted by the king.

Privately backed inquiries into agricultural conditions, particularly in the backward south, were undertaken by Sonnino, Franchetti and Fortunato. In 1877 a parliamentary commission under Jacini was set up, which reported in fifteen volumes in 1885. The condition of agricultural workers in the southern provinces of the peninsula, Sicily and Sardinia was miserable in the extreme; it was hard indeed for the inhabitants of these regions to appreciate the blessings of unification. A fundamental lack of capital did not permit the transition from subsistence farming to production for the market. The building of the Mont Cenis (1857–71), St Gothard (1872–82) and Simplon (1898–1906) tunnels, and the opening of the Suez Canal in 1869, left Italian products exposed to competition from cheaper goods, both industrial and agricultural, from abroad.

The opening of the Mont Cenis tunnel, September 1871.

Deforestation in the south led to soil erosion and an increase in the scourge of malaria. Fiscal expedients, such as the protective tariffs of 1878 and 1887, helped the more industrial north, but only damaged further the southern economy. Exports of olive oil, citrus fruits, wine and sulphur from Sicily were all badly hit in the eighties by world conditions as well as by the government's fiscal policies. Between 1886 and 1888 exports to France dropped from 500 million lire to 167 million. Social revolts in Sicily in 1893 were ruthlessly suppressed by Crispi with the use of fifty thousand troops. From 1889 a series of bank scandals, in which several prominent deputies and ministers were involved, shook confidence in the financial system and in the probity of members of the cabinet.

With government help, however, progress was made industrially after 1879: Pirelli had founded his rubber manufactory in 1872, Breda set up the Terni steelworks by 1886, Armstrong's naval yards near Pozzuoli were opened in 1885. Later were formed the great Ilva and Ansaldo groups of companies. Government subsidies helped the shipping firms of Rubattino and Florio, which amalgamated as the Navigazione Generale Italiana in 1881. From 1883 a beginning was made with harnessing rivers to generate electricity and in the following decade Marconi carried out his experiments in wireless telegraphy. The first Italian factory for making cars was established in Turin in 1895 and four years later was formed the Fabbrica Italiana Automobili Torino, better known as Fiat, which by 1914 was producing eighteen thousand cars annually.

Left: Guglielmo Marconi (1874–1937), with his 'telegraphy without wires', 1896.

Right: The first Fiat advertisement, designed by Carparetto in 1899, the year in which the firm's factory was founded in Turin.

These deep social changes were accompanied by a new awareness among the working class, who began to form associations for their protection and betterment. The Chamber of Labour in Milan was inaugurated in 1874, but was dissolved by an alarmed government. Italian idealist socialism stemmed chiefly from Mazzini and Garibaldi; the new revolutionary parties, on the other hand, had their origin in Naples in 1867, when Bakunin founded the first Italian section of the Socialist International. Marxist ideas also found early supporters and at a conference in Genoa in 1892 the new Italian Socialist Party (PSI) decided to break with the Bakunin anarchists and adopt a Marxian programme. In the nineties labour troubles became intensified, but a tendency to dogmatic hairsplitting handicapped the development of a united workers' party. In 1893 the Reggio congress of the PSI decided that socialists could sit in parliament but not vote for any bourgeois government. Gradually the distinction between a 'minimal programme' (support for reforms in existing society) and a 'maximal programme' (overthrow of the bourgeois state) was worked out.

From 1889 Crispi met the increased labour unrest, both in agriculture and in industry, by adopting powers to prohibit free assemblies and on several occasions by calling in the army. In May 1898 a violent clash in Milan provoked the army to the use of artillery to clear the streets, with the result that eighty people died. In parliament opposition from the left degenerated into obstruction and physical violence. General Pelloux, the prime minister of the right, to avoid the interminable parliamentary debates, determined to rule by royal decree, finally closing parliament amid uproar (June 1899). This arbitrary act was later declared illegal by the court of appeal. Paradoxically the consitution was ultimately saved by the action of the extreme left (the *estrema*), who walked out of the chamber. Nevertheless, the reputation of constitutional government had suffered severely. In the elections that followed, an increased number of the *estrema*, as well as of the 'constitutional opposition', were returned.

The assassination of King Umberto I by an anarchist in July 1900 may be regarded as the end of this decade of violence and social unrest. He was succeeded by Vittorio Emanuele III (1900–46). In February 1901 Giuseppe Zanardelli of the left became prime minister, with Giuseppe Giolitti in the key ministry of the interior. The succeeding period up to 1914 became known – from Giolitti's personal ascendancy and his control over parliament and electorate – as the 'Giolittian era'.

Effects of
Unification on
the Arts, Science
and Philosophy

The nineteenth century and the early twentieth, in spite of hopes raised by the *risorgimento*, and expressed by writers such as Mazzini and De Sanctis, was not marked in Italy by great originality or creativity in literature or the arts, with the exception, perhaps, of music. But even in the field of music, Bellini died young in 1835; Rossini, who lived on until 1868, wrote little after *William Tell* (1828); Donizetti died in the year of revolutions, 1848. The greatest Italian musician of the period, Giuseppe Verdi, was born in 1813, produced some of his finest operas at an advanced age (*Otello*, 1887; *Falstaff*, 1893), and died in 1901. Other popular composers of opera were Mascagni (b. 1863), Leoncavallo (b. 1858) and Puccini (b. 1858); and the Italian musical tradition was continued in Respighi (b. 1879), Malipiero (b. 1882), Casella (b. 1883), and in the conductor Arturo Toscanini (b. 1867). Of the writers Manzoni wrote little between 1827 and his death in 1870; the difficulty that he experienced in the absence of an accepted Italian language affected in some degree writers like the Catholic novelist Fogazzaro (b. 1842), the Neapolitan Matilde Serao (b. 1856), and the young D'Annunzio (b. 1863). The Sicilian novelist Giovanni Verga (b. 1840) and the novelist-dramatist Luigi Pirandello (b. 1867) won international acclaim; as did much later the Italo-Jewish novelist from Trieste, Italo Svevo (b. 1861). The best-known poet of the *risorgimento* was Carducci (b. 1835); a poet of another, more exquisite, kind was Pascoli (b. 1855); and the poetry of D'Annunzio will probably outlast his sensuously overwrought novels. Italian

Giovanni Giolitti (1842–1928), adept at parliamentary and extra-parliamentary manipulation.

painting of the nineteenth century was in the main mediocre, although some find pleasure in the work of local schools, such as the 'School of Posillipo'. Artists who later won a name outside Italy were Carlo Carrà (b. 1881), Gino Severini (b. 1883), Amedeo Modigliani (b. 1884) and Giorgio de Chirico (b. 1888). Perhaps the most influential sculptor was Medardo Rosso (b. 1858). In science and mathematics Italy had several outstanding figures, among whom should be mentioned the electrical physicist Marconi (b. 1874) and the little-known Peano, whose work on the symbolism of mathematics bore fruit in the development of modern systems of symbolic logic. In philosophy the school of positivism was challenged chiefly by Hegelian and Marxist thought, exemplified by the writings of Spaventa (b. 1817), Labriola (b. 1843), Croce (b. 1866) and Gentile (b. 1875).

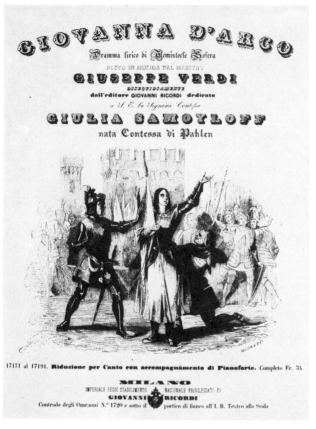

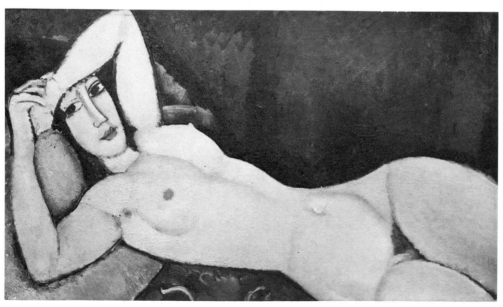

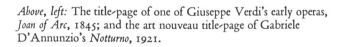

Above, left: The title-page of one of Giuseppe Verdi's early operas, *Joan of Arc*, 1845; and the art nouveau title-page of Gabriele D'Annunzio's *Notturno*, 1921.

Below, left: Amedeo Modigliani. 'Nude with Raised Arms'.

Above: Arturo Toscanini and Benedetto Croce.

Right: Luigi Pirandello.

In his attitude towards organized labour Giolitti reversed the restrictive policy of Crispi, believing that a liberal government should not identify itself with employers, but should widen its appeal to include all classes in measures of progressive reform. The number of strikes rose from 642 in industry and 36 in agriculture in 1899 to 1,851 and 856 respectively in 1901; but production also rose, and real wages. The increasing wealth of the country was reflected in a series of budgetary surpluses and by the successful conversion of the interest on the national debt in 1906 from 5 per cent to 3·75 per cent.

Giolitti's liberal reforms went far towards fulfilling the policies of moderate socialists like Turati and Bissolati, but, fearing to split the workers' movement, they refused to take office under him. The split, in fact, came from within the Socialist Party, brought about by the actions of the extreme syndicalists, followers of Labriola, who favoured Sorel's theory of revolution by acts of violence and by the weapon of the general strike. Whereas essentially practical men like Cavour, Depretis and Giolitti were frankly opportunist in their building of parliamentary majorities, the Socialist Party showed a fatal tendency to fission on points of dogma. Opportunists and dogmatists alike brought parliamentary democracy into disrespect, and ultimately the way was to be left open to fascism. The anarchists had split off in 1892; in 1908 the syndicalists seceded; in 1912 the extreme revolutionaries, among whom was the violent young Benito Mussolini, the editor of *Avanti*, gained control from the reformists; in 1915 the party was again divided on the issue of entering the war; finally, in 1921, the communists, acting on instructions from the Third International, split the movement.

In the general strike of September 1904 Giolitti simply did nothing and the strike collapsed through lack of leadership. Yet in the agricultural strikes in Ferrara and Parma in 1908 the violence of the strikers was met by violence from the now organized employers, a situation that came near anarchy in one week in June 1914, when 100,000 reservists were called up before order was restored.

Another party which advocated violence was that of the extreme nationalists, mainly irredentist and imperialist – men as different as Corradini, Papini, Prezzolini, the 'futurist' Marinetti, D'Annunzio and the 'prophet of fascism', Alfredo Oriani. Giolitti, sensing the imperialistic mood of many Italians, declared war on Turkey in September 1911, in order to secure Libya as an Italian colony. During the course of the war the islands of Rhodes and the Dodecanese were occupied and although their seizure was only provisionally recognized by the powers, Turkey ceded Libya to Italy by the Treaty of Lausanne (October 1912).

'The Fourth Estate'; strikers in 1905. Painting by Pelizza da Volpedo.

Italy on the eve of the First World War was enjoying a prosperity that was increasing annually, in spite of the labour unrest. Nevertheless, in relative figures in 1911–13 the average income *per capita* of Italians was only 158, compared with 549 for the United States and 481 for Great Britain. And even these figures are misleading, since the industrial north claimed the preponderant share, while in the south, despite the talk, little had been achieved in relieving poverty. Emigration was the only hope for thousands of unemployed or underemployed agricultural labourers (*braccianti*). In 1913 872,000 Italians emigrated, mostly to North and South America. Remittances from these emigrants were an important invisible export to the value of three hundred million lire annually, equal to the sum derived from tourism.

It was unfortunate for Italy that at the outbreak of war between the Central European powers (joined later by Turkey and Bulgaria) and the Triple Entente, the neutralist Giolitti should have been on one of his periodic planned retirements from office. Although Italy was still formally a party to the Triple Alliance, the manner in which Austria-Hungary had embarked on hostilities would have allowed her to remain neutral, which was manifestly to her advantage. The interventionists were a heterogeneous group of nationalists, irredentists, liberals, democrats, even syndicalists and socialists, among whom one of the most vociferous was Benito Mussolini, who split with his party on the question. Salandra's cabinet negotiated with both Austria and the Allies; the latter offering the higher terms, Italy signed the secret Treaty of London (April 1915) and declared war on Austria on 23 May, declarations of war on Germany and Turkey following later.

Italy gambled heavily on a victory in 1916, but when the fighting on the River Isonzo settled down to a long war of attrition, morale in the army and among the civil population was eroded, and the disastrous defeat at Caporetto in October–November 1917, with casualties of over 680,000, shook the nation. The new commander-in-chief, General Diaz, stabilized the line on the River Piave; and in October 1918, in conjunction with the Allied advance, the Italians attacked and overcame the Austrians at Vittorio Veneto, forcing Austria-Hungary to seek an armistice.

At the Peace Conference it was apparent that the clauses of the secret Treaty of London, whereby Italy was to receive not only the Trentino, Trieste and Istria, but also part of Dalmatia, could not with respect to the last point be implemented without injustice to the new state of Yugoslavia. Fiume was not an original irredentist claim, but while matters were still under discussion, D'Annunzio occupied the city by force (September 1919). The fall of Orlando's war cabinet in June of that year initiated a three-year crisis which was to destroy representative government in Italy.

The succeeding short-lived cabinets of the radical Nitti, who was supported by the Giolittians and the newly formed Catholic Partito popolare italiano, and of his successors (Giolitti, Bonomi and Facta), were unable to deal with the unprecedented economic and social difficulties arising out of the war. In the elections of November 1919 there appeared two 'mass' parties, the socialists with 156 seats and the Catholic popolari with 100 seats; together these parties represented a majority in the chamber. The socialists were deeply divided into extremists, who were much impressed by the success of the Bolsheviks in Russia (these 'maximalist' revolutionaries were to form the Italian Communist Party under Gramsci in 1921), and the reformist followers of Turati. The popolari, led by the priest Don Sturzo, although willing to join the government, were also widely divided in political allegiance.

Giolitti erred in thinking that his pre-war tactics of masterful inactivity were equal to the changed conditions. A series of general and local strikes, the occupation of the factories by workers in Milan and Turin in September 1920, the forcible appropriation of land by peasants, the participation of regular soldiers in the illegal seizure of Fiume: these events, and others, showed that

1920. A group of *Arditi*, whose name was taken from that of special shock troops who enjoyed enormous prestige as the 'commandos' of the First World War.

authority lay elsewhere than in the hands of the government. The old upholders of constitutional processes, the middle and lower bourgeoisie – professional men, the small and middle-sized businessmen and landowners – were all the hardest hit by the devaluation of the lira, the price inflation, the high taxation, and the threat of insolvency and unemployment. These persons had most to fear from a revolution, which was preached with increasing violence and which was foreseen by many as a natural consequence of the almost incessant strikes and disorders. Between the violence of the revolutionary left and of the nationalist right and the supineness of the liberal centre was to be interposed the dynamic opportunism of the unprincipled megalomaniac, Benito Mussolini.

Fascism may be said to have had its birth in Milan on 23 March 1919 at a meeting called by Mussolini to form the Fasci italiani di combattimento (Italian leagues of combat), originally a combination of diverse elements – wartime interventionists, nationalists, monarchists, anarchists, even ex-syndicalists and revolutionary socialists (like Mussolini himself). The party made little headway until the beginning of 1921, when bodies of armed fascists (*squadristi*) were employed against communists and socialists by northern industrialists and the large landowners of the Po Valley. With a cynical regard for 'realities', Mussolini, through his mouthpiece, the *Popolo d'Italia*, became the leader of the 'dynamic' party of the right. Giolitti, misguidedly thinking he could tame Mussolini, included fascists in his party lists for the elections of May 1921 (the last 'free' election for twenty-five years) and thirty-five, Mussolini among them, were elected. *Squadrismo*, with its murders and brutal beatings-up, spread over the country under the gangster bosses Grandi, Balbo, Farinacci and, when the time was opportune, Mussolini.

A series of ministerial crises produced as a stop-gap the undistinguished lawyer Facta as prime minister in August 1922. A mysterious call for a national strike gave fascists in the northern cities their awaited opportunity: they attacked the socialists in Ancona, Leghorn and Genoa and on 3 August, after street-fighting, seized and burnt the offices of the socialist *Avanti* in Milan. The government was powerless (or disinclined) to take action while the fascists took over by force key town councils in north Italy – principally that of Milan. When the fascists' plan to march on Rome became known in the capital, however, Facta went twice to the palace on 28 October to obtain the king's signature to a decree of martial law; but the king did not sign. On 29 October 1922, Mussolini was sent for by the king and commissioned to form a government. The fascist era had begun; Italy was at the mercy of her own barbarians.

The Fascist Era The record of the next twenty-one years was to give the lie to the claim for the 'moral and civil primacy of the Italians'. It is undeniable that Mussolini did have the support of many of his countrymen – at the time of the easy victory

The Lateran Treaty of February 1929, between the Italian state and the Vatican, settled the 'Roman Question', which had remained unsolved for seventy years.

over Abyssinia, the overwhelming majority. Cavour had indeed left a dangerous legacy: that reasons of state overrule all legality – and, moreover, all common morality. Yet it is not simply the criterion of success that makes Cavour admirable, Crispi reprehensible, and Mussolini despicable.

The first period of Mussolini's government was characterized by what he termed the 'carrot-and-stick' method. In January 1923 the *squadristi* were formed into the Militia for National Security, fascism's private army of 'blackshirts'. By means of the Acerbo electoral law the fascists secured a majority in the chamber at the election of April 1924. In June the socialist deputy Giacomo Matteotti was murdered by *squadristi* and his death was followed by the 'Aventine secession' of opposition members, refusing in protest to participate in parliament. A further electoral law of 1928 destroyed what little remained of parliamentary freedom by the refashioning of the chamber of deputies and the creation of the purely passive *gran consiglio*.

'Il Duce' was now free to make arbitrary and far-reaching changes in every aspect of Italian life, which was to be transformed from its roots in the creation of a totalitarian 'corporative state'. Thenceforth Italians were not required to think, since this journalistic Barnum included among his many preposterous claims to personal superiority the gift of infallibility: 'Mussolini ha sempre ragione' ('Mussolini is always right'). In speeches and from his muzzled press

◀ The so-called 'March on Rome', October 1922. In fact, Mussolini travelled from Milan by train.

he poured forth an undigested and often contradictory farrago of inflated non-sense. Nevertheless, there were few open opponents of the régime. One of them was Croce; another was Fermi, the physicist, who refused to return from receiving the Nobel prize (1938) and did important work on the atom bomb in America. Perhaps Mussolini's one statesmanlike action was in relation to the Church. By the Lateran Agreements of 1929 the 'Roman question' was settled: the Popes were thenceforth to be sovereign rulers of the Vatican City, in return recognizing the Italian state; and matters of mutual concern were duly settled.

The shelling of Corfu in 1923 had shown the 'fascist style' in foreign policy. Once secure in power, Mussolini wished to cut a prominent figure on the world stage; in 1925 he was a signatory to the Treaty of Locarno and in 1928 was a party to the Kellogg Pact to outlaw war. In the early thirties he showed himself disposed to support Great Britain and France in opposition to the uni-lateral abrogation of the peace treaties by Germany, where Hitler came to power in 1933. In Austria Italian money subsidized the dictatorship of Dollfuss; on his assassination in 1934 Mussolini mobilized troops on the border, to warn Hitler against invading Austria. Bent on war to demonstrate the virility and heroic stature of fascist Italy ('only blood can turn the blood-stained wheels of history'), Mussolini had had his eye from 1932 on Abyssinia; and at the Stresa conference (1935) he hoped to find acceptance of this proposed aggression from Britain and France in return for Italian support against a rearming Germany. The outcry which followed the publication of the Hoare-Laval plan, which would have given most of Abyssinia to Italy, disillusioned him, and he turned towards Germany. Hitler had at first warmly admired Mussolini, until experi-ence exposed the hollowness of his pretensions.

In October 1935 the Italians attacked Abyssinia; condemnation by the League of Nations and the half-hearted imposition of economic sanctions only served Mussolini's purpose by strengthening his internal position. Addis Ababa was entered early in May 1936 and on 9 May Mussolini was able to proclaim Vittorio Emanuele emperor of Abyssinia, after 'the greatest colonial war that history has recorded', won with the use of poison gas and aircraft against a virtually unarmed people. (Mussolini privately regretted that Italian losses were only 1,537, a number insufficient in his opinion to harden Italian breasts into steel.)

Taking advantage of the Abyssinian war, Germany remilitarized the Rhine-land in March 1936. In the summer steps were taken to strengthen the *rapproche-ment* between Italy and Germany, which led to the announcement of the 'Rome-

The Spanish Civil War, 1936. Mussolini addressing a crowd (only a small section of it is shown here) in favour of Italian intervention.

Berlin axis' in October, the anti-Comintern pact of November 1937, and gradually by a series of fatal errors to the quite gratuitous Pact of Steel of May 1939, which technically obliged Italy to fight alongside Germany in any war, even of the latter's making. In July 1936 Franco attacked the republican government of Spain, relying on the moral and physical support of the axis partners. By 1937 seventy thousand Italians were engaged in Spain, first 'volunteer' black-shirts, but increasingly, after a setback at Guadalajara, regular soldiers. Following his visit to Germany in the autumn of 1937, Mussolini's intoxication with the prospect of military conquest removed any judgment that remained.

In March 1938 he had to accept the *Anschluss* of Austria by Germany for the sake of axis solidarity; and at the end of the year he had so far succumbed to Hitler's ideology as to inform the incredulous Italians, the inhabitants of that much invaded country, that the purity of their Nordic Aryan blood required the introduction of anti-semitic laws. Mussolini's ambition to appear as the arbiter of nations was temporarily satisfied by the Munich conference of September 1938, at which Great Britain and France weakly surrendered to

The 'Pact of Steel' of May 1939. Mussolini and his foreign secretary and son-in-law, Count Ciano, with Hitler.

German demands on the Sudetenland. Piqued at Germany's absorption of the remainder of Czechoslovakia in March 1939, Mussolini ordered the invasion of Albania on Good Friday in the following month. In his saner moments Mussolini must have realized that Italy was in no position to fight a major war, but such moments were rare. On the RussoGerman agreement and Hitler's decision to invade Poland, which brought about the outbreak of the Second World War on 1 September 1939, Mussolini's advice or opinions were ignored by his senior partner. For the moment Italy announced her neutrality, or, as the Mussolinian rhetoric demanded, her 'nonbelligerence'.

In June 1940, when the rapid progress of German arms through the Low Countries and the British evacuation at Dunkirk threatened to end the war with a great German victory, Mussolini thought that Italy might safely attack the already stricken France. War was declared against Great Britain and France on 10 June. Mussolini, as commanderinchief, ordered Italian troops in Africa to attack British Somaliland and Egypt. By August they had taken the former, but in January 1941 ten Italian divisions under Graziani were routed by two British divisions on the Egyptian frontier and in the retreat that followed they lost 100,000 men. By March Eritrea, Somalia and Abyssinia had all fallen to the British and the duke of Aosta had been forced to surrender with nearly a quarter of a million troops.

Again, in order to rival German victories Mussolini had attacked Greece in October 1940, but after an initial gain the Italians suffered the ignominy of being driven back to the coast and ultimately of watching their German allies overrun Yugoslavia and Greece in a matter of weeks. In November half the Italian battle fleet was put out of action by the British at Taranto. So much for the

The hotel on the Gran Sasso in the Abruzzi, where Mussolini ▶
was imprisoned after his arrest on 25 July 1943, and from where
he was subsequently rescued by the Germans.

military value of unbridled rhetoric – it was Crispi all over again, but on an infinitely more disastrous scale. German troops under Rommel scored successes in Libya against the British, but Montgomery's victory at El Alamein in October 1942 and the Allied landings in Algeria brought about the final Italo-German defeat in North Africa in May 1943.

The German invasion of Russia in June 1941 and Japan's attack at Pearl Harbour in December had extended hostilities. Mussolini promptly declared war on Russia and on the United States, and sent 200,000 ill-equipped troops to the Russian front, where by the beginning of 1943 half had perished. In July the Allies were in Sicily; and at this juncture Mussolini arranged his thirteenth meeting with Hitler, but members of his own *gran consiglio* were conspiring against him. On the night of 24–25 July a motion of no confidence in Mussolini was passed by nineteen votes to seven and on the following day he was arrested by orders of the king, who appointed Marshal Badoglio as prime minister.

A pretence of carrying on the war at Germany's side gave an interval in which to approach the Allies, but by the time the armistice was agreed and announced on 8 September, German forces in Italy had been powerfully augmented, with the consequence that for twenty months Italy was a battlefield, as the Germans slowly withdrew northwards before Allied and partisan attacks. The king and the Badoglio government retired to Brindisi; Mussolini, freed by German glider troops in September ('the most romantic escape in all history'), set up the

The Resistance Movement

Italy a battlefield. The destruction at Monte Cassino.

'republic of Salò' in those northern parts of the peninsula still German-occupied. Before Italy formally entered the war on the side of the Allies (13 October), there had already begun the formation of partisan bands, who were to cause severe damage to German lines of supply and to tie down considerable bodies of troops. Over whole areas there spread all the horrors of civil war. Out of these anti-German, anti-fascist groups were formed the Committees of National Liberation (CLN), which constituted a co-ordinating link between the partisans and the resurgent anti-fascist political parties. The Neapolitans, acting in conjunction with members of the armed forces, spontaneously rose and forced the surrender of the German garrison after four days of street-fighting (28 September–1 October). The extent of civil participation in the Resistance may be gauged by the partisans' dead, which numbered over 66,000.

After the liberation of Rome by the Allies in June 1944, Badoglio's nominated government, which already included members of six parties, including Christian democrats (the successors of Don Sturzo's popolari) and communists, was replaced by one led by the reformist socialist Bonomi, who main-

The liberation of Rome by allied forces, June 1944. Crowds in St Peter's Square listen to an address by Pope Pius XII.

tained the all-party coalition. By the time of the surrender of all German forces in Italy to the Allies on 29 April 1945 most of northern Italy was in the effective control of partisans of the CLNAI (Comitato di liberazione nazionale per l'alta Italia). On 27 April Mussolini, his mistress Clara Petacci and a number of fascist officials, attempting to escape to Switzerland, were captured by partisans and summarily shot, their bodies being exposed to public abuse in the Piazzo Loreto in Milan.

One hopeful sign which emerged from the prevailing chaos was the statesmanship shown by the leaders of the main political parties, particularly De Gasperi of the Christian democrats and Togliatti of the communists. After the short-term coalition led by the ex-partisan Parri (June–December 1945), Alcide de Gasperi was appointed to the office which he was to hold in eight successive coalitions until 1953, and in which he showed a breadth of vision, constancy of purpose and political acumen unseen in Italian statesmen since Cavour. The creation of a new constitution was entrusted to a constituent assembly, elected by universal adult suffrage on 2 June 1946. King Vittorio Emanuele III having abdicated in the previous month in favour of his son Umberto, a referendum was held simultaneously with the election to decide the fate of the monarchy. A majority of two millions (12,717,923 to 10,719,284) declared in favour of a republic and King Umberto II went into exile. The results of the election to the assembly gave the Christian democrats 207 seats, the socialists 115 seats, the communists 104 seats, and the four smaller parties 110 seats. The sole threat to this Catholic democratic predominance would lie in a left coalition; the socialists, however, still suffered from the old maximalist and reformist division, the more moderate of them holding for De Gasperi. The new constitution was approved by 453 votes to 62 in December 1947 and on 1 January 1948 it came into force. In the April elections the Christian democrats gained an absolute majority over a popular front of socialists and communists. The newly elected president of the republic, the noted liberal economist Luigi Einaudi, entrusted the formation of a government to De Gasperi, on whom fell the arduous task of Italy's reconstruction.

Alcide de Gasperi (1881–1954) between members of a committee convened to discuss the setting-up of a European Economic Community.

Chapter Eight

Mussolini's misguided policy of material and intellectual 'autarky' had seriously dislocated the Italian economy and isolated Italians from the sources of much of contemporary culture. With the return to constitutional government under De Gasperi's leadership, Italy resumed her place among the comity of nations, aligning herself firmly with the industrialized countries of the West in opposition to the Eastern communist bloc. Nevertheless, Italy has the largest communist party in the West, which, under the sophisticated tutelage of Togliatti, has constantly elaborated a peaceful 'Italian road to socialism', avoiding alike the pitfalls of 'maximalist sectarianism and reformist revisionism'. After the 1948 elections the Christian democrats' majority in parliament would have allowed De Gasperi to form a single-party government, yet, true to his policy of 'centrism', he included in his cabinet republicans, liberals and Saragat's social democrats, leaving in opposition the communists and Nenni's socialists. The first major test of the government came in the debate on Italy's participation in the North Atlantic Treaty in March 1949, when, despite fierce opposition from the left, Italy's Western orientation was vindicated by a majority of two to one.

The 1953 elections resulted in a reduction in the number of seats held by the centre coalition, the gainers being the parties of the right (monarchists and the neo-fascist Italian Social Movement) and of the left (communists and Nenni's socialists). Obliged to form a purely Christian democratic government, De Gasperi was defeated in August 1953 and resigned. The prolonged series of ministerial crises which followed showed the weakness of Italian constitutional government; successive prime ministers sought a majority by moving either to the right or to the left, but any new alignment tended to split the Christian democrats. From the mid-fifties it became clear that only a movement to the left, which could draw Nenni and his socialists from their alliance with the communists, would provide a stable government. This realignment of the centre-left was achieved by Aldo Moro in December 1953, Nenni becoming deputy prime minister, with Saragat as foreign minister. More recent ministerial crises, however, have underlined the instability of the Italian party system.

One of the principal weaknesses of the state stems from the unequal development of the regions. More regional autonomy is clearly called for. In Sicily, where special historical reasons favoured the adoption of a regional administration in face of a strong separatist movement, the tradition of political anarchy, corruption and *mafioso* infiltration in many walks of public life has hindered the growth of a respect for constitutional processes. Similarly, on the level of municipal administration the record leaves much to be desired: the civic authorities of Naples, for example, have not been noteworthy for their wisdom or probity, nor can it be said that the activities of the secret society known as the *camorra* in that city have been finally extinguished.

There exists a widespread lack of confidence in the efficiency and impartiality of the bureaucracy, particularly in matters of tax assessment and in the administration of justice. In April 1970 a committee reporting to President Saragat showed that 57 per cent of civil cases were never concluded, the parties settling out of court. The reason for this is clear, for in 1965 statistics showed that the average length of a civil case was six years and eleven months. In criminal cases the average trial lasted two years and eight months; furthermore, 40 per cent of those accused were subsequently acquitted, some having spent long periods

Giuseppe Zangara, a prominent *mafioso*, shot with a *lupara* (a shot-gun used for killing wolves) outside his house in Palermo on 6 April 1961. Although his ostensible earnings had been small, he left a conspicuous legacy.

The post-war 'economic miracle'. Cooling towers at the Geothermoelectrical Power Plant, Lardarello.

in prison awaiting trial. In court procedure the absence of rigorous rules of cross-examination leads too often to the substitution of rhetoric for the patient sifting of evidence.

On the other side of the coin is the remarkable recovery of Italian industry, especially in the years 1959–64, which has become known as 'Italy's economic miracle'. From 1945 Italy has been one of the largest recipients of American aid, receiving in the period up to 1964 some 2,796 million dollars. After stabilizing the lira, the government's policy was to increase productive capacity through facilitating investment by securing international loans, by governmental grants in aid, and by private resources both internal and from abroad. From 1948 to 1955 industrial investment amounted to 85,000 million lire; for the following five-year period the figure rose to 539,000 million lire. Autonomous governmental agencies, such as the Institute for Industrial Reconstruction (IRI), the Ente Nazionale Idrocarburi (ENI) and the Istituto Mobilare Italiano (IMI) direct large sectors of the economy. For the impoverished south a special fund (the Cassa per il Mezzogiorno) has been set up to provide the capital for the rehabilitation of these, the most backward areas. A contributory factor to the 'economic miracle' was the discovery of vast sources of natural gas and of oil in the Po Valley, Apulia and Sicily, which have been successfully exploited by ENI, particularly under the able direction of the late Enrico Mattei, to provide power and the basis of a large petro-chemical industry – thus compensating for Italy's lack of basic industrial raw materials.

Palazzetto dello Sport, Rome, 1957, by P. L. Nervi and A. Vitellozzi.

Finally, Italy's inclusion in the European Steel and Coal Community (1951–52) and its evolving successor, the European Economic Community (by the Treaty of Rome, March 1957), has benefited her whole economy: for example, the Italian steel industry has trebled its capacity – at double the rate of Germany – in the first decade of the Community's existence. Between 1958 and 1961 Italy's gross national product rose by the impressive figure of 30 per cent, against 21 per cent for the whole Community. Nevertheless, in spite of the injection of huge capital sums into the Mezzogiorno, the gap between the average *per capita* income of the industrial north and that of the still primarily agricultural south (even with the construction there of large industrial complexes) has not been closed. The centuries-old 'problem of the Mezzogiorno' remains unsolved. For the year 1960 the average income for an inhabitant of the north-west was 427,000 lire, compared with a mere 177,000 for the southern mainlander.

Remarkable also has been the cultural activity of Italians since the hiatus of fascism. Novelists like Bacchelli, Tozzi and Moravia, and the poet Dino Campana, managed to have their work published under Mussolini; but the return to constitutional government brought with it a resurgence of cultural creativity, many of the novelists, poets and other writers having a strong sense of social criticism: Carlo Levi, Silone, Danilo Dolci, Calvino, Betti, Montale, Pavese, Quasimodo, Ungaretti, Bassani, Cassola, Vittorini, Fenoglio,

The ecumenical movement. Pope John XXIII (1881–1963, pope from 1958) being carried through St Peter's Square to open the Council, October 1962. ▶

Pasolini. Perhaps the Prince of Lampedusa, with his failed masterpiece *Il Gattopardo*, is worthy, too, of mention. Even more striking still has been the Italian post-war contribution to the cinema, particularly in the development from the work of the earlier neo-realists (Rossellini and De Sica among them) by such internationally known directors as Visconti, Fellini, Antonioni, Olmi and Rosi. Among painters the work of Morandi and Guttuso is widely acclaimed and among sculptors that of Marino Marini, Manzù, Greco, Morlotti and Burri. Contemporary Italian composers to win a name abroad include Dallapiccola, Menotti, Berio and Nono. Italians, with their innate sense of design, are outstanding in interior decoration and in the world of fashion. The excellence of Italian industrial design is universally acknowledged, as is the skill and taste of their civil engineers and architects. The distinctive constructions of Pier Luigi Nervi have gained him an international reputation. Despite the political uncertainty and the perhaps exaggerated pursuit of the *dolce vita*, there is no lack of evidence of a vigorous cultural revival.

With the pontificates of Pope John XXIII (1958–63) and his successor Pope Paul VI, the papacy has revealed an unsuspected capacity for renewal in order to meet the ever-changing demands of this critical age. Just as in religion Italian Popes have sought ecumenicity, so in the lay world of international relations Italians have been foremost in support of an extended European Economic Community, with its ultimate vision of a united Europe.

Short Selected Bibliography

Burckhardt, J., *The Civilization of the Renaissance in Italy* (London, 1944).

Butterfield, H., *The Origins of Modern Science* (London, 1949).

Cambridge Mediaeval History, planned by J.B. Bury (Cambridge, 8 volumes, 1911–36).

Cambridge Modern History, *New*, planned by Sir George Clark (Cambridge, 14 volumes, 1957–70).

Chabod, F., *A History of Italian Fascism* (London, 1963).

Clough, S.B., and S. Saladino, *A History of Modern Italy* (New York, 1968).

Fletcher, Sir Banister, *A History of Architecture on the Comparative Method* (seventeenth edition, London, 1961).

Jamison, E.M., and others, *Italy, Mediaeval and Modern* (Oxford, 1917).

Jerrold, M.F., *Italy in the Renaissance* (London, 1927).

Larousse Encyclopaedia of Byzantine and Mediaeval Art (London, 1963).

Larousse Encyclopaedia of Renaissance and Baroque Art (London, 1964).

Luzzato, G., *An Economic History of Italy* (London, 1961).

Mack Smith, D., *The Making of Italy, 1796–1870* (London, 1968).

—, *Italy, A Modern History* (Michigan, 1959).

Mattingley, G., *Renaissance Diplomacy* (London, 1965).

Oxford Companion to Music, The, ed. P.A. Scholes (tenth edition, London, 1970).

Penguin Book of the Renaissance, The, ed. J.H. Plumb (Harmondsworth, 1964).

Pirenne, H., *A History of Europe* (London, 1939).

Pope-Hennessy, J., *Italian Gothic Sculpture* (London, 1955).

Salvatorelli, L., *A Concise History of Italy* (London, 1940).

Saville, Lloyd, *Regional Economic Development in Italy* (Edinburgh, 1968).

List of Illustrations

38 The Emperor Henry IV. Miniature from the *Welt-chronik* of Ekkehard of Aura, 1113–14. Corpus Christi College, Cambridge. *Photo Courtauld Institute of Art.*

39 Henry IV expels Pope Gregory VII. Miniature from the *Weltchronik* of Otto of Freising, 1170. Universitäts-bibliothek, Jena.

40 Interior of a banking house. Miniature from *De Septem Vitiis*, late fourteenth century. British Museum. MS. Add. 27695, f. 8r. *Photo Mansell Collection.*

42 Masons at work. Miniature from a psalter, 1066. British Museum. MS. Add. 19352, f. 170.

43 The Emperor Lothair. Miniature from the *Psalter of Lothair*, ninth century. British Museum. MS. Add. 37768.

Eastern merchants. Miniature, *c.* 1500, from the *Nichomachean Ethics* by Aristotle. Österreichische Nationalbibliothek, Vienna. Cod. phil. gr. 4, f. 27.

44 Page from an Arabic translation of the first part of Galen's *Treatise on Electuaries*, ascribed to Johannes Grammaticus. Österreichische Nationalbibliothek, Vienna. Cod. AF. 10, f. 15.

45 Scenes of medieval medical practice. Miniature from a treatise on surgery translated from the Latin of Roger of Salerno, thirteenth century. British Museum. MS. Sloane. 1977. *Photo Mansell Collection.*

46 A Chinese mariner's compass. Date uncertain. Science Museum, London.

47 The Fourth Crusade. Pavement mosaics in S. Giovanni Evangelistica, Rome. *Photo Mansell-Alinari.*

48 Marco Polo departing from Venice. Miniature, *c.* 1400. Bodleian Library, Oxford. MS. Bodl. 264, f. 218r.

49 Edward III. Miniature from the *Ipswich Charter* of Richard II and Edward III, 1338. Suffolk Record Office, Ipswich. *Photo Courtauld Institute of Art.*

Florentine gold florin, *c.* 1300. British Museum. *Photo John Webb.*

Venetian ducat, *c.* 1280–89. British Museum. *Photo John Webb.*

51 The Torre Asinelli and the Torre Garisenda, Bologna, 1100–09. *Photo Ente Provinciale per il Torismo, Bologna.*

52 Florentines attacking Pistoia. Miniature from *Chron-ache* by G. Villani, fourteenth century. Biblioteca Apostolica Vaticana. Vat. Cod. Chigi L. VIII. 296, f. 72v.

53 Seal of the Ghibellines. Obverse and reverse. Museo Nazionale, Florence. *Photo Pineider.*

Seal of the Guelfs. Obverse and reverse. Museo Nazionale, Florence. *Photo Pineider.*

54 The Emperor Henry IV asking for the Countess Matilda of Tuscany and Abbot Hugh of Cluny to intercede for him with Pope Gregory VII. Miniature from the *Vita Mathildis*, early twelfth century. Biblioteca Apostolica Vaticana. MS. Lat. 4922, f. 49r.

55 *Prestanza* cover with the *gonfalone* of the Whip of the Quarter of Santo Spirito, Florence, 1408. Archivio di Stato, Florence. *Photo Pineider.*

56 Rome. Fresco by Taddeo di Bartolo, 1414. Palazzo Pubblico, Siena. *Photo Ente Provinciale per il Torismo, Siena.*

57 The port at Pisa. Relief, late thirteenth century. Museo di Architettura e Scultura Ligure, Genoa. *Photo Direzione Belle Arti, Genoa.*

58 Façade of the Cathedral, Pisa, 1063–92. *Photo Edwin Smith.*

59 The royal court, Palermo. Miniature from the *Liber ad honorem Augusti* by Petrus de Eboli, 1195–96. Bürgerbibliothek, Bern. MS. 120/II, f. 101.

The Emperor Frederick Barbarossa. Miniature, twelfth century. Biblioteca Apostolica Vaticana. Vat. Lat. 2001, f. 1r.

61 King William II of Sicily presenting a model of Monreale Cathedral to the Virgin. Mosaic, twelfth century. Monreale Cathedral. *Photo Mansell-Anderson.*

62 Pope Innocent III. Fresco, thirteenth century. The Lower Church of Sacro Speco, Subiaco. *Photo Alinari.*

64 Officials of the Merchants' Guild. Miniature by Sano di Pietro from the *Statuto della Mercanzia*, Siena, 1472–75. Archivio di Stato, Siena. *Photo Grassi.*

65 Persecution of the Waldensians. Engraving from *Histoire générale des églises évangeliques des vallées de Piemont ou vaudoises* by Jean Léger, 1669. British Museum.

66 St Francis of Assisi. Fresco, *c.* 1220. Lower Church of the Sacro Speco, Subiaco. *Photo Alinari.*

67 St Dominic presiding over a court of the Inquisition. Painting by Pedro Berruguete, late fifteenth century. Prado, Madrid. *Photo Mansell-Anderson.*

69 The Emperor Frederick II. Plaster reconstruction of the head from the Triumphal Arch at Capua, 1235–40. Museo Campano, Capua. *Photo Lala Aufsberg.*

Gold *augustale* of Frederick II. Obverse and reverse, 1220–50. British Museum.

70 Castel del Monte, Apulia, *c.* 1240. *Photo Lala Aufsberg.*

71 Right and wrong way to hold a falcon on horseback. Miniature from *De Artibus venandi cum avibus* by Frederick II, 1248. Biblioteca Apostolica Vaticana. MS. Pal. Lat. 1071, f. 89v.

74 Charles of Anjou, king of Naples. Sculpture attributed to Arnolfo di Cambio, 1277. Palazzo dei Conservatori, Rome. *Photo Mansell-Alinari.*

75 The battle of the Maccabees. Miniature from the *Arsenal Bible*, 1250–54. Bibliothèque Nationale, Paris. MS. Arsenal 5211, f. 339.

76 Note of payment by the city of Lucca to Sir John Hawkwood and his mercenaries, 7 October 1376. Archivio di Stato, Lucca.

Index

*Page numbers in italics refer to
illustrations*